FROM ZERO TO SIDEMAN

in 5 steps

Mel Brown

Illustrations by Doug Bale

Career Equity LLC

Unlocking the value of experience.

From Zero To Sideman In 5 steps By Mel Brown

Copyright © 2008 by Mel Brown

Illustrations: Doug Bale

ISBN: 978-0-9815706-0-0

Editor: Chuck Vermillion, Helppublish.com

Additional Editing by Michelle Conley

Interior Design and Cover Production: Yvonne Vermillion, Magicgraphix.com

Printed in the United States by Lightning Source www.lightningsource.com

Published by Career Equity LLC, Gilbert, Arizona

For information about Career Equity LLC
and to report errors email: zero2sideman@mac.com

．．．

This book is dedicated to my Mom, Beatrice Brown, who told me that I could do anything I put my mind to. Hey, Mom! Guess what? I taught myself how to play the bass...figured out how to get a gig...invented a whole new way for musicians to market themselves...went on tour...recorded on #1 records... won a Grammy...wrote a book...

and realized that I have the best Mom in the world. Thank you!

．．．

. . . .

ACKNOWLEDGEMENTS

I'd like to thank:

James Bilodeau for his article, "The Simple Steps for Starting Your Own Publishing Company, and Marketing Your Own Book – Masters of Our Own Destiny" which provided the mechanism to bring this book to you.

Doug Bale for his excellent illustrations, outstanding talent, and great attitude.

All of my close friends who had to endure my talking about this project for over a year.

Alex Manzanares for his assistance, ideas, and support in the making of this book.

Jay Piccurillo, Rich McDonald, and all at Fender.

David Lienhard and all at Dean Markley.

Bill LaCommare and all at Interactive Solutions.

The staff at the San Tan Apple Store in Gilbert, AZ.

Chuck and Yvonne Vermillion at helppublish.com and Magicgraphix.com

Darlene Rahn for her help editing and great advice.

. . . .

TABLE OF CONTENTS

FROM ZERO TO SIDEMAN (IN 5 STEPS)

If you're reading this book, then you're probably interested in learning about Sidemen, becoming a Sideman, or upping your game as a Sideman. Whatever your preference, you came to the right place. This book can help you do all three.

You've probably never heard of me, and you need to know who you're getting this information from, so I'll start by giving you some relevant info about myself:

- My name is Mel Brown, and I'm a professional Sideman (bass player) from Denver, Colorado.

- I quit my day job at age 25, moved to a major music city four years later (Los Angeles), and successfully injected myself into the music scene in less than 3 weeks.

- I was the first musician in the world to use an Enhanced CD-ROM as a business card. I handed out my first one in Los Angeles in October 1997, and I still use it to promote myself.

- My musicianship and self-promoting efforts have appeared in *Bass Player, Bassics Magazine, Global Bass, Fender Frontline,* and other magazines.

- I've toured, performed, and recorded with major Artists, including Brian McKnight, Marc Anthony, Gladys Knight, Kenny Lattimore, George Benson, Al Jarreau, Jeff Lorber, Monica, Eddie Murphy, Chuck Loeb, Wayman Tisdale, Joey DeFrancesco, Kenny Loggins, Michel Camilo, Toby Keith, Brian Bromberg, and others.

- I've recorded mostly on Smooth-Jazz projects, several of which were number one CDs, number one radio singles, and dozens of top 10 projects.

- I played bass on the song that won a Grammy Award for Best Pop Instrumental in 2006. The song is "Mornin'" by George Benson and Al Jarreau on their duet project called *Givin' It Up*.

- I've appeared on camera for major TV shows, movies, and commercials for the last fourteen years.

- I have endorsements with Fender Bass Amplification and Dean Markley Strings.

- I've done clinics at the School of Bass in Arizona, The Los Angeles Music Academy, and the University of Southern California.

- I have a web site (www.melbrown.net), and everything you need to know about me as a Sideman is there, including how I started, the projects I've played on, and videos of a few performances. I hope you will log on, check me out, and say "Hi" in my guest book. You can feel free to drop me an e-mail at any time, too.

Now that you know a little bit about me, I'll tell you why I wrote this book. I've been fortunate to have done some cool gigs in my career and love sharing my experiences with other players. I'm always being asked questions, from how to get an endorsement to what strings I use. I'm happy to share information, but time usually runs out before I've shared it all. Sometimes musicians will invite me to hang out so they can "pick my brain". I'm cool with that, too, and even though I look forward to getting together, I rarely have the time to hang out, so it rarely happens. That is why I wrote this book. Here in these pages is the information I'd share if we got to hang for a few hours, for the same price you'd pay a decent teacher for a private lesson or to buy me some Italian food for lunch (my favorite!). This book is better than taking me to lunch, though, because you can read it as much as you like and I won't gain any weight. Another reason for this book is that you won't learn much of this information at a traditional music school. I find it sad that so many students get their music degree but have no clue about how to get a gig. I'm also amazed at how many musicians believe that there's some "dark secret" that holds the key to breaking into the music industry.

I'll be setting up a web site (www.fromzerotosideman.com) to go with this book. The site will have forums, articles, and other relevant Sideman information that you probably won't find at a music school. I hope you come away from the book and the site able to advance your Sideman career.

I'm not one to waste time, so let me start by giving you an outline of what I'm going to share with you:

From Zero...

You're reading this section right now. The goal here is to introduce myself and affirm that you're getting this information from a musician who walks the walk, talks the talk, and lives the life of a bona fide Sideman. I've done the stuff you're going to read about here, and my growing career is proof that my methods work. Since I'm a bass player, the book reads from that perspective, but anyone seeking a career as a Sideman can benefit from this information.

The rest of the book contains five sections that present a simple and practical method for chasing success as a Sideman in any city with a music scene. By "simple", I mean "easy to understand" not "easy to complete". Success in any endeavor requires hard work, and being a Sideman is no exception. You should keep in mind that my methods are not the only way to get your career going; they are simply one combination of actions that have worked for me. If you have a better way to achieve success, then have at it! If not, here are my five steps with brief descriptions:

1 – Choose the Life

Choose the Life means deciding to be a Sideman with your eyes open. This section defines what a Sideman is, what a Sideman does, and more importantly, what a Sideman isn't. I'll also show you where Sidemen fit into the music industry as a whole. After that, I'll shine the light on some realities that no one warned me about — realities that you should consider before you decide to become a professional Sideman. I know I probably didn't think of everything here, but these thoughts should be more than enough to get the wheels in your mind turning.

2 – Equip Yourself

The best work happens when you have the right tools. Here you'll find suggestions on selecting and buying the computer gear and musical gear necessary to chase success as a Sideman. Most players have gear before they choose music as a vocation. I'll share some experiences here that will give you an idea of whether you should continue building on what you've got — or if you'll need to rethink your choices.

3 – Educate Yourself

Here I offer some straight talk about learning your craft as a musician. I touch upon reading music, playing by ear, tablature, private instruction, books, learning songs, technique, researching gigs, and more. Here you'll find some practical suggestions about how and where to start learning regardless of where you stand as a player. By the way, I don't recommend military bands as an avenue to getting educated. That's because the name of my book is From

Zero To Sideman not From Zero To Deadman. There is always the possibility of war these days and I'm not comfortable suggesting that someone's kid take that risk. There are suggestions about a few practical skills outside music that you should develop, too.

4 – Make a Demo

It seems that everyone has a different opinion about what should or shouldn't be in a demo. There are no basic standards or guidelines for making demos, for their content, or even a universally accepted format in which to present them. I'll show you how to make the perfect musician's demo similar to the one I successfully used to introduce myself to the music industry in a major music city — Los Angeles, California.

5 – Self-Promote

Many musicians don't exactly know what self-promoting is or how to go about it. Other musicians do a poor job at promoting themselves, because they don't view it as an important or necessary part of their careers. Solid self-promotion can help you advance your career quickly, and here I'll share some of my own proven methods on how to do it. I also talk about networking and how it can impact your career, too.

...To Sideman (Time to Go to Work!)

If you've done the work in these 5 sections, you'll be getting calls and should be well on your way to having a career as a Sideman. I offer some closing thoughts about why you'll get calls, what to expect on your new gigs, and some tips on keeping it together when you're the newbie.

This seems simple enough, right? I'm starting from zero, which means I'm assuming you know nothing about being a Sideman. That way I won't leave anything important out. Let's get it going with "Choose the Life".

set goals
define success
?
choose the life

CHOOSE THE LIFE

Based on my own experience, I believe that most people outside the music business (I'll call them "Music Civilians".) hold a common notion that there are two kinds of musicians — famous musicians and struggling musicians.

The famous musicians incite fascination, adoration, and garner sincere respect from Music Civilians. This is because famous musicians perform at large places, are covered by popular mass media, and they are inaccessible to the public. Reality shows, such as VH1's Behind the Music, often reveal that many of these characters start off as good folks just trying to "make it" and end up as self-destructive victims of their own success, often in rehab or broke. Nevertheless, the fascination, adoration, and sincere respect for these characters are unaffected.

On the other hand, the struggling musicians incite pity. These musicians are readily accessible, work in nonmusical professions, and they're rarely showcased in any media. Music Civilians view a career in music as foolhardy, with heartbreak and disappointment at the end of the road. If the subject of music as a profession arises in a conversation, Music Civilians almost always know of a failed or struggling musician. I hear them put on a somber tone of voice when they mention:

- "That young woman at work who has a beautiful voice and maybe even a music degree, but she never 'hit the big time'. Instead, she sings in the church choir or in a hotel lounge."
- "A cousin who's so talented but abused drugs or alcohol and could never 'turn the corner' with a career in music."
- "That friend who had a bad experience in the music business, gave it up, and now works as a frustrated professional."

Sadly, most people view struggling musicians as the norm, which can be a huge discouragement to the fledgling player. Folks still look at me apologetically after learning what I do for a living — then they put on their most polite but obviously dismissive and pessimistic tone and ask me, "Are you in a band?" These same folks are always pleasantly surprised (though embarrassed) after further conversation reveals the depth of my involvement, my honors, my knowledge of, and, yes, my obscurity in the music industry. Their early condescension and cynicism for my job gives way to fascination and admiration as they learn more about my place in the music industry. You see, I'm not a famous musician or a struggling musician; I'm a musician who:

- Occupies the huge middle ground between the legions of famed and failed musicians.
- Continues to be an essential driving force in the music industry and its economy, despite being mostly ignored by the media and the public.

- Can enjoy a thriving career spanning many years in an industry where Artists who seek fortune and fame arrive today and vanish tomorrow.

This musician is called a "Sideman", and I'm currently enjoying a successful career as one of them.

What is a Sideman?

To understand what a "Sideman" is, one has to understand what an "Artist" is first. In the music industry, an "Artist" is the main attraction, the main character, or the main performer on any stage. That stage can be at a neighborhood bar, on a movie set or video shoot, at a recording session, in a gazebo at an outdoor wedding, on the main stage at Madison Square Garden, or in a garage. An Artist can be a singular person with one or more talents, such as a vocalist, instrumentalist, composer, actor, poet, comedian, a group of two or more people, or any combination of these. Some examples of singular Artists are people such as Beyonce, Madonna, John Mayer, Sarah McLaughlin, Kenny Chesney, Garth Brooks, Vince Gill, Alan Jackson, Joey DeFranceso, Mike Stern, Christina Aguilera, Brittany Spears, Eminem, Herbie Hancock, Snoop Dogg, Dianne Reeves, Carlos Santana, Josh Grobin, LL Cool J, Tupac Shakur, Biggie Smalls, and others. Anyone else performing onstage with any of these singular Artists is called a Sideman. Some examples of popular Artists that are groups are The Rolling Stones, Pearl Jam, Nirvana, G-Unit, Red

Hot Chili Peppers, Green Day, Third Eye Blind, Brooks and Dunn, Charlie Daniels Band, Vertical Horizon, Foo Fighters, Metallica, Gnarls Barkley, The Police, Kiss, Rush, Van Halen, Earth Wind & Fire, Cameo, Destiny's Child, SWV, or the Ohio Players.

Sometimes the name of a group features the name of one member to distinguish that person as singularly important, while recognizing a consistent group of musicians as being an important part of that act or sound. Names such as Diana Ross and the Supremes, Martha and the Vandellas, Gladys Knight and the Pips, Huey Lewis and the News, Tom Petty and the Heartbreakers, Christie Hynde and the Pretenders, Prince and the New Power Generation, or Doyle Bramhall and Smokestack are examples that come to mind. In these examples, the Vandellas, the Pips, the News, the Heartbreakers, the Pretenders, and Smokestack are also all considered Artists. Anyone who is not an official member but performs onstage with any of these groups is a Sideman. Artists who are groups are less likely to employ Sidemen because they are usually self-contained, but it happens. Darryl Jones replaced Bill Wyman in the Rolling Stones but is not a member of the group. When John Entwistle suddenly passed away in 2002, The Who finished their tour with Pino Palladino.

Simply put, a Sideman is a supporting character to an Artist on any stage. Even though a Sideman can have many of the same skills as any Artist, the role of a Sideman usually begins with one core skill (such as playing bass or singing behind an Artist). If the Sideman has other skills, such as playing other instruments or dancing, their role may be adjusted accordingly by the Artist. There are no limits to how a Sideman's role can be defined by the Artist.

There are a few more important differences between Artists and Sidemen to be noted here. The Sideman's name is almost never seen on flyers, advertisements, show tickets, or on the marquee outside the venue. Sidemen are only employed to do tasks the Artist can't or won't do themselves onstage, and we make a lot less money than the Artist.

Some Sidemen can and do become famous in their own right and go on to be Artists themselves. George Michael, Luther Vandross, Sheryl Crow, Doyle Bramhall, Marcus Miller, Stanley Clarke, and Paula Abdul are some examples. Each one of these people started their career by playing, singing, dancing, producing, writing, or performing behind other Artists. As their skills improved and they became more sought after by various Artists, they began to use their credibility as Sidemen to forge opportunities for themselves and achieve success as Artists. Even as their success as solo Artists grows, some of these folks I just mentioned are still working as Sidemen.

Other Sidemen get together and form groups that achieve commercial or critical success. Toto, Steps Ahead, and Fourplay are some examples of this. They, too, are able to enjoy success as Artists while keeping creditable careers as Sidemen. A group like the Traveling Wilburys would not be an example of what I'm talking about here, because Bob Dylan, Roy Orbison, Tom Petty, and George Harrison are all Artists in their own right.

Now that you understand what a Sideman is, let's take a look at what we do to earn our money.

The Work of a Sideman

What follows is a list of the work that Sidemen do to earn a living. I made this list before I ever quit my day job so I could keep track of what work was available, who was doing it, and for me to aim for some of it. This list hasn't changed much over the years, and you can use it as a starting point for finding work in your town:

Live Playing

This is the most common and plentiful work available to Sidemen. A simple definition of live playing is showing up at a location with the necessary equipment and performing live for a fee. (Note: "Live" usually means in front of an audience, but these days, an audience is optional and doesn't always happen.) Many live playing events are televised, broadcast on the radio, or sent out over the Internet, but most are not.

There are three types of live playing that a Sideman can do.

1. **Cover Bands** – Groups of two or more musicians who specialize in performing or "covering" material from popular Artists. Their instrumentation, content, and style may vary, that is, they may play some Rock, Pop, Swing, Jazz, and then mix in a little Funk. Some cover bands may specialize by

performing Adult Contemporary, Country, Grunge, or Metal exclusively. Others may be even more specialized — only performing songs by some of Pop culture's most famous Artists such as Elvis or The Beatles. I've worked with bands that perform material exclusively from time periods such as the Motown Era, the 80s, or the 90s. These tribute bands also often require their members to look and dress the part.

2.   **Original Bands** – Artists or Groups with two or more musicians who perform their own material. This is a lot more common in major music cities, but these gigs are everywhere. You can find them if you know where to look.

3.   **Solo** – Performance with only one or two people playing and singing, or even just playing. I've done solo gigs where I played the melodies and solos on the bass and my iPod provided the band. I guess you could say that I'm temporarily an Artist when I'm doing these gigs.

Unless you live in a major music industry town, most live playing occurs with cover bands performing cover material at different places for different purposes. Here are the places I found and probably the ones that you'll find in your town:

Playing In Church

Many players get their first live playing experience in church. Most church bands I work with perform material from popular Modern

Christian or Gospel Artists like Fred Hammond, Gary Oliver, David Crowder, Skillet, and others. Original songs are rare. I recognized, gravitated toward, and accepted the blessings these positions provided — spiritual guidance, a steady weekly income, valuable live playing experience, and recording opportunities. In other words, I'd get the Word and some Bread. I'm just kidding! Well, not really...

There were also several networking opportunities, because even the most inaccessible people come to church and talk to the band. Some churches recognize musicians as professional contractors and pay them for their services. They couldn't care less where you played the night before, as long as you meet their professional standards and reasonably uphold their social standards. (A conversation about this could fill an entire book!) Other churches know that religion is a powerful and persuasive social entity, and they use it to pressure musicians to play for free or "for The Lord". I religiously avoid these churches. Some church leaders frown upon playing "secular" music and regularly use their influence to discourage their musicians from performing at bars and clubs. The key here is to be honest with yourself, to decide where religion fits into your life, and to decide what your boundaries are with church requirements — then decide what's best for you.

Food & Beverage

I refer to playing live for local gigs at restaurants, bars, coffeehouses, hotel or private club lounges, malls, local arts festivals, or public performances for those who pass by as "Food & Beverage" gigs. These gigs often provide most of a Sideman's income, will typically last two to four hours, and can go as late as 2:00 a.m. I was visiting New York City in '95, and there were gigs that started at 2:00 a.m.! This was also the case at a few casinos in Las Vegas.

General Business

I call playing live at weddings, receptions, private parties, and other celebrations such as proms, Bar Mitzvahs, corporate trade shows, award dinners and banquets, conventions, and country club annual meetings "General Business" gigs. I call them "General Business" gigs because they usually come through an agency that provides entertainment contracting services to prominent meeting and event planners. Agencies such as Bob Gayle in LA, Bruce Garnitz in LA, Pro Entertainment Network in Denver, or Moments Notice in Denver are all examples. There are always a few business-savvy bandleaders who get this work independently, too. Performing with these bands is demanding, because their repertoire often runs the gamut with styles and time periods. I've never performed a single original piece of music at one of these gigs. These agencies can have a single band or several bands with multiple configurations, and they might also handle the contracting of other entertainers such as clowns, dancers, fire-eaters, magicians, comedians, mimes, or strippers. They also book gigs in other states and abroad. Working for these agencies or bandleaders is often more profitable than Food

& Beverage or Church gigs, but these gigs come with inconveniences such as:

- Early set up – These events are usually formal and don't allow for equipment to be moved in or set up while the event is going on. Sometimes a band must finish setting up several hours before the performance. If the gigs are far from home, you regularly have several hours to kill. This can be a real drag if the gig is at an exclusive country club, because you may have to leave the building until show time.

- Strict dress code – I don't know about you, but I HATE wearing a business suit or a Tuxedo while I play bass. But, hey, no one wants some guitar player walking around their formal event wearing jeans and a T-shirt.

- Remote locations – I'm always amazed when someone wants to be wed on the side of a mountain with a live piano player to play the march, or when someone expects the band to play in the middle of a grassy field after two days of rain.

- Snob Factor – Event planners use the agencies because the clientele is sensitive and doesn't respond well to people outside their comfort zone. Receiving "less than elite" treatment by wealthy individuals or their handlers can be trying to a Sideman's patience. Sometimes these people oversee everything, from where you enter the building, your movements, your performance, and your parking, and even which restroom you can use. You're watched by people whose only purpose is getting a tip or getting rid of you. Having a solid inner peace and a strong sense of self-worth can go a long way if you do these gigs regularly. These gigs can be cool, because they often end early or pay overtime when they run late, and there's rarely a problem with getting paid.

Touring

Many musicians hear this word and immediately associate being "on tour" with "making it". I used to think the same — but now that I know the truth, let me clear this up for you. "On tour" only means "traveling with" an Artist, original band, cover band, or some company to different cities or towns to do some live playing. The people you're "on tour" or "traveling with" may drive an old beat-up van, have terrible hygiene, and sleep in the parking lots of fleabag roach motels. They could also be the original Artist who just sold a million copies of their CD. An example of being "On Tour" with a company or group could include a circus, a band of gypsies, or a cruise-ship line. The point is that simply being "on tour" is not a symbol of success on its own. Touring is simply a combination of traveling and live playing. It can be well paying and fulfilling or a textbook example of sacrificing yourself for your art.

Sidelining

These are gigs where musicians work as actors in TV shows, advertisements, or movies. The roles are always comparable to what musicians do in real performances. These gigs can occur in cities where television or movie productions are happening. I'll give you few examples of sidelining gigs that I've done so you get my point.

- Turner Classic Movies produced a TV ad for their movie guide called "Now Playing". The scene was a 1930s nightclub with a small Jazz combo. I was the acoustic bassist in the band. This commercial is still on the air after twelve years.
- Universal Pictures made a film called *The Flintstones: Viva Rock Vegas*. I played the role of a left-handed prehistoric electric bassist playing in a Rock Vegas hotel lounge.
- Universal Pictures made a film called *The Nutty Professor 2: The Klumps*. I played the role of a bassist in a wedding band at the end of the movie.

In terms of hours, these gigs are the most time-consuming but can pay residual income for several years. You might be on the set at a sidelining gig for twelve hours waiting to shoot a 2-minute scene, but that scene may be shown on TV around the world for twenty years. Regular participation in these gigs will require you to join a performance union such as SAG (Screen Actors Guild) or AFTRA (American Federation of Television and Radio Artists).

Plays or Musicals

Playing in the pit for musicals is another professional playing opportunity. Check out *Sweeny Todd, West Side Story, Funny Girl, I'm All Shook Up, Godspell*, or *Oklahoma* for examples of this kind of work. Tyler Perry has also done several outstanding musicals that are worth taking a look at for this kind of work. Sometimes these shows have a self-contained band that travels — but other shows pick up players in each town. These gigs can be challenging musically but provide better hours than most other gigs, and they pay better than most local gigs you'll find.

That covers just about everything with live playing. Let's talk about another aspect of a Sideman's work — recording sessions.

Recording Sessions

A bare-bones definition of a recording session is "For a fee, you're hired to play someone's song and you allow someone to record you while you do it." Recording sessions can be for Artists, other Sidemen, advertisements, television, film, radio, etc. There are basically three kinds of recording sessions:

1. Traditional Recording Sessions: Musicians travel to a recording studio to record on a project. These studios can be large, well-equipped facilities or a small project-based room in someone's house. I've done traditional recording sessions at large studios in Los Angeles, New York City, Atlanta, Nashville,

Toronto, Denver, Japan, Arizona, and at some of my friends' smaller home-based project studios.

2. On Location Live Recording: Video or audio of a live performance is captured for airing as a TV show, or for release as a live CD or DVD. *The Tonight Show with Jay Leno, The View,* and the *Today Show* are all examples of TV shows. *Marc Anthony's The HBO Concert,* Keiko Matsui's *White Owl,* and BJ Putnam's *Live at CFTN* project are examples of live CD or DVD projects that I've done.

3. Remote Recording Sessions: Sessions in which producers, Artists, and musicians record their parts in separate studios and then exchange sound files over the Internet or via overnight mail. I make most of my income from recording in this way. Producers and Artists e-mail their tracks to me; I record my bass to their music, and then I upload these tracks to an FTP space where they can be retrieved. Clients pay me electronically or by a check in the mail.

Recording can be profitable in several ways, because it provides a documentation of your skills that lasts forever and is promoted by others. Copies of recorded projects often find their way into the hands of people you don't know which can generate more work for you. Recording on TV and film sessions can be lucrative, because the Musicians Union has a special payments fund that pays royalties on work for years after it's done. For the local Sideman who mainly plays live, recording sessions are a prime opportunity to earn more money while avoiding scheduling conflicts with their live playing, since session work can happen during the day.

You should take note that recording sessions and live playing are two different disciplines, and the musicianship required to be a session player (a.k.a., "Studio Musician") is significantly higher. This is because of the need to deliver an acceptable performance of unfamiliar material in a relatively short period of time, and individual performances are often thoroughly inspected by producers for quality. Studio musicians rarely know what's going to happen at a traditional session, but their reputation is always riding on how quickly they can make a previously unheard composition sound like music. They may have to create a part, read a part, or learn a part by ear. Someone might even sing a part to them. Anyway, they must be able to assimilate the information quickly and turn it into a stellar performance. I refer to this as "Arrival Time" — the time between when a player first hears the track or sees the sheet music and when the track sounds like music. The shorter the Arrival Time, the better.

Writing and Producing

Composing (writing), arranging, and producing music for Artists or other businesses is a great way to create long-term residual income and commands substantially higher fees than just being a Sideman. Being a composer, a producer, or a writer is beyond the scope of this book, but it is a real alternative to aim for as an addition to being a regular Sideman. If you have the ability to get along well with others, manage projects, hire musicians, write arrangements, and operate recording gear (or if you're willing to pay someone to do these things) you could pursue this.

Solo Projects

If you have the talent, the interest, and the resources, you should also be a Micro-Artist. "Micro-Artist" is a term I created for this book. It means that you're not trying to hit "The Big Time" but that you do have your own original project which you can sell at your Sideman or Solo performances. You may even book some of your own shows or be the opening act for "Superstar P" as well as playing behind them. I've seen some Sidemen do this effectively to advance their careers and increase their income. I've learned that audiences always admire and respect everyone involved in a good performance, and if given the opportunity, they will express interest in supporting a Sideman's career — "You sounded great! Do you have your own project?" That moment represents an opportunity to sell your CD. At the top of the Sideman's world, my friend and vocalist Arnold McCuller sells his own CDs while performing on tours with Artists such as James Taylor, Bonnie Raitt, and Phil Collins. Here, in Phoenix, my friend Rachel Eckroth sells her CDs at her performances with Khani Cole.

Teaching

Teaching others has always been a way for professional musicians to supplement their income. Unfortunately, many musicians spend most of their time learning to play and little or no time learning to teach. If you decide to teach, I'd suggest taking lessons from a great teacher before you do. Strong communication skills, patience, organization, a solid curriculum, and a sincere desire to share information about your craft are necessary to be effective here. You should be specific about selecting or rejecting students. Ask yourself if you want to teach beginners who can barely hold their instruments, adults, or advanced college students.

If you don't really know your craft, do us all a favor and stay out of this part of the industry. This book represents my first effort to teach seriously. I hope you use this knowledge throughout your career and continue to learn after reading it. Being a clinician at a high school would also fall into this category.

Transcriptions and Copyist

Having the ability to hear music and write it down for yourself or others to read is an invaluable skill in this business. Besides being an excellent way to supplement your income, to bolster your reputation, and a major time-saver in preparation for your performances, transcribing is also the fastest way to improve your musicianship. I take great pride in the charts I write for the gigs I do, and I've sold them to others for profit. This skill is not mandatory, just highly desirable and marketable.

Career Equity

Career Equity is another term I created for this book and for the name of my publishing company. It's the value of credibility gained from your previous success and experience. This credibility can be used to create new opportunities and revenue. Randy Jackson was a Sideman who "found" Mariah Carey. He used that experience to land jobs at record labels as an A & R person, to qualify himself for finding new talent on *American Idol* as a judge, and to write a book about what it takes to be an Artist. An accomplished player might write a book about how to play scales, how to improvise, or even how to become a Sideman. Instructional DVDs also fall into this category.

Other Skills

There are an infinite number of other skills outside the music industry which can be employed to supplement your income as a Sideman. If you do web-site design, you can offer this service to other musicians. If you know the tax laws, you might offer some consulting services to musicians around tax time. If you're an expert at using certain gear, you might demo products at trade shows or retail stores. If you're a great writer, you can write a book about how to be a Sideman and sell it to musicians for the price of a private lesson or a nice lunch. You might also write a regular column for a popular music magazine like *Downbeat* or *Modern Drummer*.

Some of you may be looking at my list, scratching your heads, and saying, "Is that it? I can't buy a Mercedes teaching kids where 'G' is on a bass! I don't want to spend the rest of my life in the suburbs playing at churches, bars, or weddings with regular folks like Mel Brown! I'm trying to take it to 'The Next Level'! I want to pick and choose my gigs like SuperSidemanX. I want to roll up in my Fat Ride to be interviewed like Saw-him-in-the-magazine Sideman Y. I want to play in the Big Sessions like Read-his-name-in-the-credits Sideman Z."

I understand. I hope you make it there. But for now, let's keep it real and practical. Even better, let's talk about what you may have heard or imagined about successful Sidemen at "The Next Level" and put it into the proper perspective.

"The Next Level"

Though details vary from player to player, we've all heard stories and rumors about that famous utopia of status called "The Next Level". For years, players have been romanticizing and fantasizing about "Making it" to this Next Level and what it might look like in terms of lifestyle, material satisfaction, public praise, and respect from their peers. Sometimes I'll be talking to a player and they'll be asking me questions about some other aspect of being a Sideman, but I can tell that all they really want is confirmation of The Next Level's existence. They can't figure out why it's so elusive and why so few musicians achieve it. I let them know that I understand by telling them a little story about a fictitious bassist who's at The Next Level. It goes like this:

The Baddest Mofo, a Few Days in the Life of a Top LA Bassist,
By Mel Brown

It's early morning in Los Angeles, and the sun is just starting to burn away the cloud cover. You thought you were dreaming, but you realize the phone is ringing. You answer it and learn that "Well-Known-&-Respected-Sideman T" can't make a session date and gave your unlisted number to "Unfamiliar-But-Very-Important-Person K". K needs you to come in at the last possible minute and save his session by sight-reading a song called "Looks Like Flyshit On Paper And Grooves Like The Quintessential Gospel Soul".

You were enjoying some of the best sleep of your life, and you feel like you could take it or leave it, but then K says the magic words, "The money is outrageous." Your attitude changes, and now, despite being groggy-eyed, you're willing to make the date and be the hero. You hit your cartage guy, Oscar, on his cell. Oscar knows that you'll be playing your butt off and once again solidifying your position as "The Baddest Mofo in LA" and offers to grab you a coffee on his way to the session.

After a quick shower and a 20-minute ride, you roll your late model 7 series BMW up to the security gate at Super Big Studios. The guard is expecting you (of course) and greets you by name. You spot Oscar near an open parking space holding the Special Diva Chocolate Mocha you "so desperately need" to throw down the gauntlet on some music this morning. The two of you share pleasantries, and while he's leading you to the studio where you'll record, he asks which bass you'd like him to have ready for the gig later that night.

Confused, you ask, "What gig?"

Oscar replies, "Playing in the House Band at the Grammy Awards taping — it's tonight."

You're surprised because you'd actually forgotten! Right then, you bump into Speven Steilberg, a filmmaker who's on-site checking on the progress of his latest movie's soundtrack. He says he needs you later in the week, confirms your number, and tells you to expect a call Thursday morning.

You enter the studio for your session and notice that folks are obviously nervous about you filling in. This is an important session, so they called "Well-Known-&-Respected-Sideman T" first, and they don't know you. You quickly put everyone at ease with your cool, witty, and confident manner. You quip that K rousted you out of the best sleep of your life, but you assure them that all is cool as you grab one of your three custom-made signature axes. You ask to hear the track while you take your first look at the chart. The engineer gets a level on you while you blaze through the chart and make notes. You notice those folks in the back are already impressed and starting to relax. The music is serious (technically challenging, deep in the pocket, and soulful too!), but you understand what's happening, and you realize you're about to knock this one out of the park on your first swing.

You slyly ask if you can just go for a take and see what you get. The engineer starts the track, and, yes, you absolutely kill it the first time around. The vanishing nervous energy, the shocked-but-pleasantly-surprised smiles, and a small round of applause all suggest that the ball flew over the wall and someone's windshield is smashed.

Now K is whispering your praises to "the money guy" in the back of the room. He's probably bragging that he knew how good you were all along, that he knows twenty other guys like you, and that the guy would be smart to call him for all of his future projects. It's all good though — because you're about to make K look good by showing off a little. You're lying in the weeds, about to ambush these poor defenseless Suits with some of the most potent musicianship they've *ever* seen or heard!

You quip, "Save that take, because it's only going to get worse! There's no way I can do that again!" The room bursts into laughter as the track rolls again. You really let them have it now — the full-size economy jug of 'WhoopAss' with 25% more 'Free WhoopAss'. You're playing some seriously extra-tasty stuff and still catching everything on the paper.

The producer smiles and says, "I think we're done," and about 45 minutes after you arrived, you're exchanging pleasantries, thanking K for the call, and heading for the door.

But your show's not over — you tell Oscar, "Bring these three axes to the gig tonight," within earshot of K and the rest of the folks.

After all, this is LA, and you know someone will ask, "What're you doing tonight?"

You nonchalantly answer, "Some TV show . . ." and hurry out the door. You know that Oscar will fill in the blanks, adding more amazement to your knockout performance and garnering even more reverent praise and respect in your wake. Back on the boulevard in the BMW 7, you hit T on his cell, thank him for the call, and assure him that everything went well. He says he's on the *Grammy Show* tonight and that drinks are on him.

You return home to find messages from Superstars X, Y, and Z. They're all anxiously awaiting your decision about joining their world tours (for outrageous money, of course) but you'll get to those later today — maybe. You want to stay in town doing sessions for now. You also hear messages from Producers A, B, and C. They all need you for their recording projects, because, "You're just what the project needs — and by the way, the money is outrageous." You decide to return those calls first.

You realize that you only have a couple of hours before you've got to be onstage for the Grammy's, so you grab a quick bite, clean up, and head over to Paper Clip Center in Downtown LA, and a few hours later, the show has gone off without a hitch. You've added about twenty household names to your resume, nabbed some camera time, and the Musical Director for the show has asked you to put next year's show on your calendar — in ink.

You head out to one of the many swank after-parties in a real tony section of Beverly Hills and hang out with Sideman T and the Stars until the wee hours. You go home and fall into the best sleep of your life, but soon the phone rings; It's Speven Steilberg's assistant:

"Is this The Baddest Mofo?"

You: "Maybe. Who's asking?"

Assistant: "Are you available to speak to Mr. Speven Steilberg?"

You: (Rubbing your eyes and clearing your throat) "Yes."

Assistant: "Excellent! Please hold one moment, Mr. Mofo; he'll be right with you."

Another chipper voice appears on the phone. It's Speven Steilberg.

Steilberg: "Baddest Mofo! Steilberg here. I know I told you Thursday, but things have changed, and I really need you to help me out of a jam over here at Super Big Studios like, right now. Can you come down?"

You: "Sure man! No Problem!"

Steilberg: "Man, that's great! Listen, I know it's early so the session is catered. I really owe you one, and I'll see you down here AS SOON AS POSSIBLE! Hold for my assistant!"

The assistant returns to the line: "Mr. Mofo?"

You: "Yes?"

Assistant: "This project is important to Mr. Steilberg. What will you need for compensation to come down?"

You: "I'll need the Full-On-$tupid-Na$ty-Bank, plus cartage — and your personal phone number."

Assistant: "That's excellent, Mr. Mofo, but Mr. Steilberg was thinking closer to THE-$ERIOU$LY- FRICKIN'- OUTRAGEOU$- NEXT-LEVELI$H-NA$TY-DOUGH, plus cartage. Since our number is greater, why don't we just go with that?"

You: "That will be just fine."

Assistant: "Wonderful, Mr. Baddest Mofo. We're happy to be working with you, and I'll be seeing you here at Big Studios as soon as possible. Thanks again, and good-bye!"

Just as you hang the phone up, it rings again. Even though you don't recognize the number, you pick it up. It's Steilberg's assistant calling from her personal cellphone!

Assistant: "By the way, my personal phone number is (818) ***-****! You really are the Baddest Mofo!"

You're still smiling as you slide behind the wheel of the BMW 7. You hit your cartage guy on his cell. He, knowing that you'll be grooving your butt off and once again solidifying your position as The Baddest Mofo in LA, offers to grab you a coffee on the way . . .

. . .

Okay, so I decorated it a little more than I should have. But it's still a good story, and you would be surprised at how many players fantasize about living their lives like this after they graduate from whatever Big and Famous Music School USA. They ask me questions like, "Who do you know that's on that level? What are they like? Have you been to their house?" Then they get really serious and say something like, "So, Mel, now you can be honest with me. After hearing me play, do you really think I can make it to that level? What are my chances? What should I work on? What should I do first to make it happen?" Here's the answer for all of you.

To even have a shot, you have to take a hard look at your own Big Picture and choose to be excellent in every aspect of it. That means excellence in your musicianship, professionalism, self-promotion, gear, integrity, location, knowledge of the industry, self-discipline, etc. Take a minute and ask yourself, "Have I worked hard enough to be excellent in every one of these areas?" I've met musicians who have a chip on their shoulder because they think they're not getting their due. They believe their talent is overlooked, that the industry has somehow shortchanged them, or both. But after hearing them play or after hearing them talk for a few minutes, it's painfully obvious why they're not where they want to be with success or in life in general. If you're one of these players, you need to know that your circumstance will always tell the truth about your choices — even if *you* won't.

Let's assume you've taken a halfhearted or lazy approach to learning music and your musicianship is lacking. One day out of the blue you'll notice that you're mostly performing and sought by other musicians whose musicianship is lacking. Now let's assume you're unprofessional and without integrity. You'll soon recognize that most of the musicians around you share those traits. If you choose to be a crack addict, you'll eventually look around and notice that your friends are all addicts and that you're losing gigs. Suppose you live in Poe Dunk Small Town away from civilization and choose not to network with folks or live in a city where you could earn a living as a player. There would be no possibility of a Speven Steilberg calling you at the last minute — and if it happened, you couldn't make it to the gig anyway. Take a hard look at your attitude. Are you too negative? Are you a complainer? Are you a bitter and cynical jerk? I don't care how well you play, most great players won't want to be around you if you are, and that lessens your chances of making it to that Next Level.

The same is true if you overemphasize one area of your Big Picture and neglect others. You'll be the guy who knows how to get gigs but plays poorly. You'll be the guitar player who brings eight guitars and a rack to the coffee shop gig. You'll be the guy with the PhD in music education who hasn't heard of Stevie Wonder and doesn't know a single one of his songs. To even have a shot at reaching Baddest Mofo-type success, you'd first have to choose excellence in every aspect of your Big Picture.

Another truth is that you won't be high rolling like the Baddest Mofo if you're a Sideman who only plays General Business gigs. Instead, you have to keep a healthy mix of work types. I've met some Sidemen who do have a life similar to the "Baddest Mofo" who prove this point. Randy Jackson comes to mind. Marcus Miller is another great example of a Sideman with Baddest Mofo-like status. These guys have done well because they choose excellence in every aspect of their Big Picture, and they both have a good mix of work types that they do to earn money.

To help you understand this concept, I'll give you a simplified example to show where most Sidemen fit in the music industry. Then, using Marcus Miller as an example, I'll explain how he got to that Next Level by choosing excellence and by keeping a healthy mix of work types.

Music vs. Widgets

The truth is that the music industry is just like any other industry — instead of making widgets, automobiles, MP3 players, or shoes to sell to the public, we make songs. It's important to see where you exist in the process of making songs and on the income ladder as a Sideman. I'll compare songs and MP3 players as an example to show my point:

Step #	Songs	Process Name	MP3 Players
1	Jack comes up with a great idea for a song.	Original Invention.	John comes up with a great idea to organize and use songs by employing digital technology.
2	Music and lyrics are written down.	Invention Documented.	An illustration of the device is drafted with a description.
3	A demo of the song is recorded.	Prototype.	A functioning prototype of the device is built.
4	Adjustments are made in song to suit taste and purpose.	Product Development.	Changes made to improve functionality and quality.
5	Copyright applied for. Song renamed if necessary.	Protection of Intellectual Property.	Patents applied for and device renamed if necessary.
6	Big Label pays Jack a fee and Song placed with recording Artist on their roster.	Licensing.	John sells rights to market and sell MelMP3 to Fruity Computer Company.
7	Song introduced to industry folks, retailers, and limited public by listening parties, radio, Artists appearances.	Market Analysis.	MelMP3 introduced to industry folks, retailers, and limited public via trade shows.

Step #	Songs	Process Name	MP3 Players
8	Final version of song mixed, mastered, duplicated, packaged, and placed with retail outlets for sale to the public.	Mass Production/ Product Launch.	Final version of MelMP3 enters production at manufacturing facility in China, packaged, and placed for sale to the public at leading retail outlets.
9	Song is a hit! Sells Millions of copies!	Sales, Recoup Investment.	MelMP3 is a hit! Sells millions of units!
10	Effort to increase sales of Song through live performances and mass media advertising.	Marketing and Sales.	Effort to increase sales of MelMP3 through mass media advertising.
11	Jack and Big Label Get **PAID** They've made it to "The Next Level".	Huge Profits.	Fruity and John Get *PAID** They've made it to "The Next Level".
12	Process starts again, this time with Big Label paying Jack a large fee to engage.	Initial Investment.	Process starts again, with Fruity Computer Company paying John a large fee to engage.

Now, about distributing profit for each product, I'll show you where Sidemen fit in this scenario:

Who Makes the Big Money?

Songwriters and Inventors (Like Jack and John). Owners of companies, who are willing to risk investing in each product, (like Big Label and Fruity Computer Company). Sidemen who are involved in this part of the industry and understand how to get paid are here.

Who Makes Really Good Money?

Owners of Retail Outlets, TV, Radio, Print Media, Ad Agencies, and Manufacturing Companies are here. Sidemen who earn more than standard royalties by direct selling of the product through their web sites, selling at shows, and are consistently busy performing in multiple styles are here, too.

Who Makes Better than Average Money?

Executives responsible for carrying out ideas of the owners above are here. Sidemen who rarely share in the writing of songs but have a good mix of work types and are consistently busy in multiple styles are here.

Who Makes Average Money?

General Managers who are responsible for managing day-to-day for The Executives. Sidemen who mostly play live but otherwise don't have a good mix of work types and are not actively self-promoting or performing outside a specific style.

Who Makes Below Average Money?

Employees who handle physical assembly, point-of-sale transactions, demonstrations, transport, or provide the service related to a product, etc. Musically incapable Sidemen who are ignorant as to how their industry works are here. Sidemen who don't self-promote and are not viewed as viable or preferred Sidemen for work are here, too.

Who Makes Low Money?

Those who physically maintain the facilities needed to run the business, those who handle cleaning, repair, grounds keeping, etc. Rookie Sidemen are here.

Granted, this is an oversimplified and general example, but I hope you'll still get my point. If you think about my "Next Level" story, you'll find that the main ingredients needed for The Baddest Mofo to live that grand lifestyle are flawless musicianship, a market for his service, and making a lot of money.

Now, look at my oversimplified example above and think about where a Sideman can make money. If the Sideman only appears at steps 3 & 4 (playing on demos or master sessions) and 10 (playing live gigs), that wouldn't be much income in the grand scheme of things. If you consider the entire music industry, these are not the highest paying steps to be involved with. The most successful Sideman's position in the music industry is at the top or the "upper middle". These Sidemen are involved with more than a few important aspects and styles of music in the industry, and their reputations continue to lead them to similar opportunities. The Rookie Sidemen, barely getting by and trying to make a name for themselves, are near the bottom and comparable to the "Low Money" category. The drug-addicted, socially inept, or otherwise incompetent Sidemen will eventually end up here too. Trust me.

Now, look at the steps where the big money is potentially changing hands. At step 6, John or Jack got an advance payment in exchange for Big Label or Fruity Computer Company to market and sell their intellectual property. At step 7, John and Jack should receive a royalty or compensation of some kind for every MeIMP3 made or every CD printed. At steps 8 & 9, John and Jack have the opportunity to collect on any sales-based incentives because MeIMP3 or the song was a hit with the public. At step 12, Big Label and Fruity Computer Company are pleased with the money they made, and they're willing to pay Jack and John Big Money to invent similar products or improve their original products. Their motto is, "If it worked once, it'll work again!" This effectively also makes Step 1 a moneymaker. As you can see, involvement with these other steps enables you to benefit from the success of the industry as a whole and not just a small part of it.

Now I'll explain why Marcus Miller made it to The Next Level. In other words, if you're looking at my oversimplified example above, he's taking part in all the other steps in the music industry as well. We don't even have to take an in-depth look at his career to see what should be obvious to anyone seeking success as a Sideman in this business:

- Marcus is one of the most sought-after Sidemen in modern music. His musicianship is impeccable. He's also involved with several styles of music, so he appears often in steps 3, 4, and 10.

- He creates songs and secures copyrights for his Thriller Miller publishing company, so he's involved in steps 2 and 5.

- He earns income from hundreds of songs placed with Artists and released by labels, so he's involved in steps 6, 7, and 8. He's also involved heavily and commands reasonable fees for producing music he didn't write.

- Some of these songs are hits to varying degrees, so he appears at steps 9, 10, 11, and 12, which leads to folks at Big Labels to ask him to do it again. Back to step 1.

- Marcus has joined forces with companies such as Fender Musical Instrument Company, EBS Sweden, and DR String Company to make products like the Marcus Miller Signature Bass (Fender) or to market products (EBS, DR Strings). He also has various products for sale on his own web site. These products include T-shirts, hats, CDs, DVDs, and other products. Marcus tours extensively in support of his own projects as an Artist, furthering commerce on his web site, and making new opportunities. Can you understand why he's at The Next Level now?

I'm here to tell you that being a Sideman almost never leads to the high-flying lifestyle that we see on *MTV Cribs* or *Lifestyles of the Rich and Famous*. If you're looking to hear your name with Robin Leach's famous accent, then you should probably choose something else to do. If you'd like to do well as a Sideman, then you should consider choosing excellence in all that you do and keep a healthy mix of work types like Marcus does. Being a Sideman can provide a good lifestyle (I earn quite a bit more than the median income in the US.) but you'll have to know what you're getting into and adjust your expectations accordingly.

At this point, I hope you have a clear picture of what a Sideman is, how we make money and a little understanding about our place in the music industry. But there's more to consider if you want to make an informed decision to be a Sideman.

Living the Life of a Sideman

Many people fail to realize that their occupation is directly related to their lifestyle. This often leads to choosing a career for the wrong reasons, which leads to disappointment, discontent, poor performance, and ultimately, failure. The same holds true for choosing a career as a Sideman. Before you jump into this, you should get to know the industry as much as possible through reading books, asking other musicians, and doing your own research. Then you should carefully consider how this industry can affect your day-to-day life. What follows are a few of the basic realities in the life of a professional Sideman and a brief description of what those realities could mean to you. Obviously, everyone is different, and you might think of some issues that I don't discuss here. My goal is to get you thinking and inspire you to look further.

Choosing a Career as a Sideman Means Choosing Self-Employment

Choosing to be a Sideman is essentially the same as starting your own small service-oriented business. That means you're responsible for properly setting up the business with a Tax ID number, a trade name, and a bank account. You'll also handle all the day-to-day details for this business. Besides those responsibilities, you'll also be the person providing the services to your clients. Running your own profitable business isn't easy, so don't take this lightly. If done correctly, your business could sustain you and then some. You won't need an MBA, but you should have some understanding of how to run a small business before you do it. If you are computer savvy and have Internet access, go to www.Google.com and do a search under "Starting your own business" to find a wealth of free information written by experienced entrepreneurs from all over the world.

If you don't know about protecting yourself and your assets from possible litigation by using a LLC, contracts, and insurance policies, then being a self-employed musician may not be for you. If you're not willing to pay someone to handle these tasks, you might want to choose a different career.

Marketing & Self-Promotion

Take a minute and think about the last time a vacuum cleaner salesperson knocked on your door. Remember what you thought? It was something like, *Why don't you get lost,* or, *I never should have opened the door.* Remember how your goal was to get rid of the person as soon as possible? Do you remember how committed you were to preventing the salesperson from demonstrating the vacuum in your home? Well, guess what? This is how other musicians will view you when you introduce yourself as a Sideman and invite them to hire you. The fact is, if you want to be successful, you have to constantly get the word out about your business. This is called 'Self-Promotion', and you'll have to do it on some level throughout your career. Whether it's spreading the word by meeting people, by handing out a simple business card, by owning an elaborate web site, or any combination of these things, self-promotion is essential to maintaining a career as a Sideman. Take it in! Accept it! Get in to it! Then get good at it! I offer some solid and proven tactics for promoting yourself later in this book. If you're not comfortable with promoting yourself, or you are unwilling to pay someone to help you with this, then being a Sideman is not for you.

Money-Management

I saw several talented musicians come to LA, only to leave before they could get anything going. They didn't lack talent, but they couldn't manage their finances in a way that enabled them to stay in town long enough to make anything happen. This is another reality of being a Sideman that you'll have to deal with — managing your money during economic ups and downs in the industry. Unless you enjoy living hand-to-mouth, one of a Sideman's most important tasks is to fiscally insulate yourself from the downs. These economic downs happen when:

- Work is slow or sporadic, and competition for that work is fierce.
- Your clients take their sweet time to pay you. (I performed on Soul Train and the checks came eight months later!)

- Your clients don't pay you at all and you have to become a collection agency.

The ability to pay your bills on time during periods of misfortune is a must. If you're not good at managing money and you're not willing to learn or pay someone to do this, being a Sideman may not be for you. If you don't know the law or your rights, or you're not willing to familiarize yourself with some of the recourses available to you when you get stiffed, becoming a Sideman may be a bad idea. If you're not willing to deal with these situations, don't get into this business, because they are going to happen more than a few times in your career.

Taxes

This is where people from all walks of life commonly fail to educate themselves, and Sidemen are no exception. When you're an employee for "Company X", your income is steady and the pay is consistent. You're usually paid with one financial instrument, a check. At the end of the year, you receive your W-2 and you use the information on it to file your taxes. While I don't claim that preparing any tax return is simple, understand that preparing your taxes from a single W-2 is a lot easier than preparing your taxes as a self-employed business owner. If you're a Sideman, you may have to accept various financial instruments. I've accepted U.S. and foreign currency, traveler's checks, personal checks, promissory notes, and even pennies as payment for my services. You also have to be ready to prepare your taxes as a sole owner of your business or as the manager of your LLC. At the end of the year, you'll receive a separate statement from every person or business that paid you more than $599 that year. Some businesses will report your income as if you were an employee. Others will send you a form called a 1099 or any number of other forms available to them for tax reporting purposes.

Ignorance of the tax laws can result in paying too much money to the IRS or worse, an audit. If you're audited, you'd better be ready to deal with them by having organized records and a solid accounting system in place. A mileage log for your car, depreciation and cost of repairs on your equipment, deductions for expenses that you've incurred during the normal course of business, and losses from nonpayment, are all items the IRS might examine. If you're unwilling to become knowledgeable or pay someone to prepare your taxes, then being a self-employed Sideman isn't for you.

Being a Sideman Means Being Gone

Being a Sideman can also mean not being home, and that means not having any consistent time to spend preserving relationships, homemaking, having pets, or being involved in lasting local commitments. This may not seem important to you at first, because you're so anxious to get on the road and go "on tour". I have to admit that I didn't miss anything or anyone from home when I first went on the road. That changed drastically when my wife and I had children. Looking at your tour book that contains four months of dates can be devastating when your baby son screams every time you put him down, and your teen-aged daughter asks you with her eyes and a silent bad attitude to stay home. It's also a lot to ask of your spouse or partner to manage your household alone, take care of the kids alone (a.k.a. being a single parent!), and essentially live alone while you're globe-trotting, helping "Mr. Bigstar" or "Ms. Flavor of the Month" further their careers. Another unforeseen disappointment that I experienced was seeing life at home move on without me while I was gone. My daughter had new and cool "teenage slang" and gave me the "D-uh" when I had to have it translated. She grew up while I was gone, and missing that remains the biggest mistake I've ever made. My baby son took his first steps while I was onstage in Tampa, Florida playing behind an Artist who

I didn't even like or respect. My old friends had new friends and new endeavors, and their personalities had changed — so had mine. In less than two years, many of us had lost touch and grown out of what we once had in common. I also noticed the calls to go out for coffee, a pickup game of basketball, or to see a local band stopped coming. My friends had grown tired of wasting their time checking to see if I was home and had begun to assume that I wasn't. To them, it didn't matter if I was playing with a critically-acclaimed Jazz musician or with a certified superstar; to them I was just "unavailable" or "gone". So they moved on, and I didn't blame them.

My wife had gotten used to having total control of the TV and actually scowled at me when I came home and picked up the remote! That's when I had to make a change! I'm just kidding about that being the reason I decided to get off the road. But that is a true story. Overall, the effects of seeing the people in my life moving on without me made me take a hard look at my career choice. I won't even begin to talk about trying to keep a romance going while one of you goes on the road. It's cool for the first week or two, but then your significant other turns on the TV and sees you onstage with the hot dancers around week nine. Then you miss their call at 1:00 A.M.; that's a recipe for The-Full-On-Maximum-Drama-Breakup Fight. You're headed for a breakup with five weeks to go on the road! Or worse, your partner comes out to meet you on the road — and the relationship goes south when they assume that you could easily replace them with a different person every night in any city. I speak from experience — be careful what you wish for, and look before you jump.

Being a Sideman Means Living Opposite to the Rest of Society

For many people, this could mean a full-scale lifestyle change.

- On Monday morning at 7:00 A.M. when most people are dreading rush-hour traffic, the Sideman is still snoozing.
- On Friday evening, when most people are dreading the rush-hour traffic and heading home to enjoy the weekend, the Sideman is just getting ready for work.
- On holidays, when most people are looking forward to quiet family time, the Sideman is heading out for a gig that pays a little bit better than most others.
- It's the weekend, Saturday night, or New Year's Eve (take your pick), when most people are lining up outside the club waiting to socialize and party the night away, the Sideman is trudging through the kitchen to the stage for work.
- Later that night, when most people are stumbling home, getting laid, getting arrested for DUIs, or heading for another club, the Sideman is loading his gear back into the car, getting paid, and heading home to unload his gear yet again.
- It's Sunday morning, and most people are donning their Sunday best for church, trying to sleep off the hangover, or

making Sunday breakfast before the Big Game. The Sideman has, after 3.5 hours of sleep, been rehearsing with the church choir for at least an hour.

- When most people are entertaining family or watching the Big Game on Sunday afternoon, the Sideman is struggling to stay awake or stealing a nap before heading off to the occasional Sunday night gig.

If you're not comfortable living opposite to the rest of society as I've just described, then being a Sideman is not for you. If you need to look at what everyone else is doing to verify the validity of your own actions, then being a Sideman is not for you. If you love your spouse or significant other, and that person isn't comfortable being with someone living and working opposite hours, I strongly recommend that you reevaluate whether it's worth it to pursue this career. You should think long and hard about how your absence at holiday events, (social gatherings, family gatherings, or family events, because of your work schedule) will affect you and those around you. Then you must carefully decide whether it's a circumstance that you and your partner could continuously deal with. By the way, working several days a week at bars or clubs where drunk "hotties" regularly offer you a good time is enough to test the mettle of any relationship. I've seen some good Sidemen go down in flames when that "Nice Hot Chick by the Bar" turned into the "Crazy Cold Stalker by Their Car".

Being a Sideman Means Defining Your Own Success

Before you choose to be a Sideman, you should define what success would look like to you in terms of musical ability, personal satisfaction, material satisfaction, and income. Be specific and realistic! Some of you may think this is corny, but I speak from experience when I say that setting specific and realistic goals for yourself is the most effective first step to achieving success in anything. You might even think of it like this:

Specific + Realistic = Attainable

Being specific and realistic gives us well-defined responsibilities, enables us to measure our progress toward completing them (accountability), and insulates you against failing before you start. Being "specific" and being "realistic" always go hand-in-hand, and if you want to do anything, you should never have one without the other. Here are some examples of goals that people set for themselves and shared with me at their lessons:

Example 1 – Specific and Unrealistic:

"I want to be Getty Lee, on a sold-out world tour earning $1 million yearly, own several luxury cars, and appear on *MTV Cribs*. I also want to re-record the 'Exit Stage Left' live record and play some different bass licks on 'YYZ' and in the solo section on 'Freewill'!"

Explanation – These goals are all specific, but they're an obvious recipe for failure. No matter how hard you try, you can never be another person or re-create that person's original creative works better than they did the first time. These are not goals, they're pipe dreams. They're ideas that can't and won't ever become realities. Goals can become realities — pipe dreams can't.

Example 2 – Nonspecific and Realistic

"I want to hit the big-time so I can be in charge of running things, have money, tell people what to do, and be at the golf course while answering important calls on my cell phone!"

Explanation – these statements are just pipe dreams too, because they only highlight the effortlessly-achieved and totally fabulous results of some nonspecific endeavor. They offer no details about what product or service will be marketed or sold to achieve the success (no work). They're also vague and generalized at best (no responsibility or accountability required). They're only realistic in that they allude to a stereotypical idea of what a "successful" person does.

What exactly is the "big time" and how do you know when you've "hit it"? What are you doing to "hit the big time"? Eating hot dogs? Posting handbills? Cleaning chimneys? Selling vacuum cleaners? Investing? What "things" would you "be in charge of running", and how much money does it take for you to feel like you "have money"? Who exactly is on the other end of that "important call" on your cell phone?

Example 3 – Nonspecific and Unrealistic

"I want to be the Bill Gates of the music business and have everyone else looking up to me as an example of their potential success. My company will set the tone for the entire music industry within the first year of operations!"

Explanation – I nearly died laughing when a 36-year-old man actually tried to hustle me with this one. He got mad when I encouraged him to be specific by asking, "How do you want to be the Bill Gates of the music business? What will your company do or make? Are you going to invent some tool or process that will revolutionize how the industry does business, and, if so, what is that tool or process? Will you sell your idea to a specific company or license it to a bunch of companies in the music industry? Speaking in business terms, one year is not a long time. How will you know that your product or process is revolutionary and is needed by the music industry?" By this time, he was ready to leave and had gathered his belongings. I told him to enjoy his pipe dreams, but to call me when he wanted to get serious about his musicianship. As you can see, no further discussion is necessary for "goals" like these. Without any specific service, skill, talent, or process preceding them, they are simply BS.

My Own Goals

When I seriously decided to pursue a career as a Sideman, my mom agreed to let me live rent free at her house for one year. I stood up and walked out of my full-time job at a Denver bank. Now I'd done it. I had 365 days to launch my Sideman career. I had to get organized and set some specific and realistic goals. Below are some of the goals and my definition of success that I wrote down when I was 25 years old. I'll share these so you don't have to figure out what goals to set for yourself — you can use mine as a guide.

My Musical Ability

I'd like to quit my day job and be able to rely on my musical ability and knowledge to earn my living and be well respected by my musical peers. I've seen others do this in town, and I'll find out how much education they have and start by mirroring that. I'd like to be sought after and perform on the most coveted gigs in town. That means I'll have to learn, be able to understand, and accurately perform all the songs at those gigs. I'd like to maintain a large repertoire of songs that would enable all the bandleaders in town to use me on bass. I'd like to be comfortable while sight-reading any piece of sheet music placed in front of me and be able to transcribe songs accurately by ear. I'd like to feel comfortable playing bass solos and "faking" on any song. I'd like to have a firm understanding of music theory and its practical application in my day-to-day musical life. I'd like to develop and maintain a high level of technical and physical ability on my instrument.

My Income

I'd like to earn between $70,000 and $150,000 yearly throughout my career. I've met musicians who proved to me that they earn this, so I know it's possible.

I'd like to invest in a 401(k) and an IRA, have six months of reserve cash in a savings account, and a better than average health insurance plan.

I would like to have satisfactory insurance for all of my assets, personal and professional.

My Material Satisfaction

I'd like to own a large home in a low-crime suburban neighborhood. I want to be near excellent schools in case I decide to start a family. I'd like to own a quality car that's less than five years old to drive to my gigs — and a luxury car for my personal life. I'd like to have a well-equipped home studio where I can practice, work, and manage my career. I'd like to have an excellent selection of instruments and effects at my disposal to explore and use. I'd like to have a stylish wardrobe, comfortable shoes, cool sunglasses, and maybe a couple of nice watches.

My Personal Satisfaction

I'd like to perform on a major tour and be well paid for playing to a sold-out crowd at Madison Square Garden. I'd like to make a name for myself recording on Pop Instrumental or Smooth-Jazz projects with as many Artists as possible. I want to play bar gigs with the guys who are on some of my favorite records. I'd like to experience what life is like on a tour bus and see as much of the world as possible before I settle down into a marriage and start a family.

Exit Strategy – If I can't get a career started within this year, I'll find another job and aim for higher education. I define a career as working as a full-time musician in the Denver area, with consistently growing prospects and opportunities to perform or record nationally or internationally. I'm 25 years old now, and I'm going to pursue these goals until I'm 35. When I'm 35, I'll evaluate my progress. If I'm successful, I'll continue with my Sideman career. If not, I'll either get a 9 to 5 or go back to school. No matter what, I intend to stop traveling when I'm 35 and settle down.

After you define what your own success looks like, you should immediately find out whether that success can be partially or fully achieved if you remain in your current city or town. If you live in a music city such as New York or LA, you won't have to move. Otherwise, you may have to move like I did to achieve your goals. You should look around at the musicians in your area and see whether any of them have achieved success similar to your goals and study how they keep it going. Start asking yourself some tough questions, and keep it real when you answer them. Are you married to a stay-at-home wife, with two small children, a dog, two cars, a mortgage, and using an excellent health care plan provided by your day job? If you are, now may not be the best time for you to quit your day job, move to a new city, and start a new career as a Sideman. On the other hand, if you're single, with no debt, and have low overhead expenses, a move to a major music city could be the best choice for you.

Assess how important your goals are with regard to your current situation, and adjust them as necessary before you decide to move to a new city or stay where you are. The methods outlined in this book will help you rise to the top of the pile of Sidemen in your area no matter where you live.

As for me, I decided that I could achieve most of my goals in the Musical Ability, Income, and Material Satisfaction categories in Denver, but some of my goals in the Personal Satisfaction category required a move to a major music city such as Los Angeles. Even though I was afraid to move, I was unwilling to forgo these satisfactions to avoid moving. I wanted to "play local gigs with the guys who are on some of my favorite records" and to "play a sold-out show at Madison Square Garden and be paid well to do it" — both of which required a move. The best information I had was that most tours were originating in LA. Since I was 25, single, and didn't have any children of my own at the time, I finally decided not to forgo any of my goals in the Personal Satisfaction category, and I moved there. My short-term goal was to focus on my Musical Ability goals in Denver and then chase the rest of my goals in LA.

Setting goals was the only way to hold myself accountable for progressing or achieving success in my endeavor to become a professional

Sideman. Starting a new career at 25 is considered late, so I had to make up for lost time. I organized, set my goals, and got the work done. I also defined an exit strategy that clearly said what my actions would be if I succeeded or failed. If you are unwilling to define your goals and hold yourself accountable for consistently working toward them, then being a self-employed Sideman may not be for you.

Being a Sideman is Cool

But take heart, Sideman-wanna-be! Choosing to be a Sideman or any other career is not all bad, and I want you to know there are many positives. The following are some highlights of my life as a Sideman.

- Remember the song I played on that won the Grammy Award for "Best Pop Instrumental"? I recorded it in my pajamas with my son on my shoulders! Three of my favorite Bassists are on the album (Marcus Miller, Stanley Clarke, and Abraham Laboriel), and my song won!

- I rode the "Midnight Train" to Georgia and did "The Bump" with Gladys Knight.

- I played my bass in front of sold-out crowds at Madison Square Garden — and made great money to do it.

- I sang and successfully butchered the song "Back at One" while Brian McKnight played my bass and cracked up laughing.

- I enjoyed watching my son's face when he saw me standing alone on the big screen dressed like a Flintstone.

- I've stood on the big screen next to Eddie Murphy while he portrayed one of the Klumps.

- I've opened *Radio & Records* and saw that I had played my bass on 4 of their top 10 Smooth-Jazz songs.

- I've seen my name in the credits next to some of my heroes like Marcus Miller, Abraham Laboriel, Stanley Clarke, Will Lee, John Pattitucci, Michael White, Poogie Bell, Michael Landau, Chuck Loeb, Bubba Bryant, Vinnie Colaiuta, and others.

- I've set foot in every state and relaxed in some of the most exclusive hotels. I've snoozed on some of the most exclusive beaches in Palm Beach, St. Maarten, and Maui, to name a few. I've been paid to tour London, Spain, Paris, Ireland, Singapore, Puerto Rico, Japan, Canada, The Bahamas, the Canary Islands, and South Africa.

- Now that I'm off the road, I'm free every morning to help my son get ready for school. I ride bikes with him to and from school, help him with homework, attend parent-teacher conferences, and most of all, I'm there for him during those all-important hours between 3:00 and 6:00 P.M. I wouldn't trade this for the world — or for a world tour.

- I consistently earn more than enough money to afford an upper-middle-class lifestyle.

If you're not sure or have doubts about being a professional Sideman after reading this chapter, you should probably quit now (or just play music as a hobby), because it only gets harder from here. If you choose to play music as a hobby, some of the methods in this book can help you get the most out of that, too. You still need to keep it real though — if you think you can do this with no inner conviction, no musical ability, no talent to build on, or if you just plain suck, this book won't help you. Do yourself and the rest of us a favor then — just walk away! If you feel empowered by this information and want to give it a shot, then Choose the Life and let's go gear shopping!

EQUIP YOURSELF

Buying a Computer for Your Digital Life as a Sideman

If you're going to be a Sideman, you've got to have a good computer. Players ask me what computer I use and what I'd recommend to someone in the market. Until now, I've always expressed that Macs are the best but that we live in a Windows world. Now, Macs are simply the best computer that money can buy. I'll tell you what I have, why I have it, and what I recommend if you are in the market for a computer now.

What I'm using

I have an older Mac (OSX, 750MHz PPC, 2GB RAM, with two 300GB 7200RPM Seagate drives). I have 2 Intel based Macs that run Mac OSX and Windows XP. A Mac Mini (1.8 GHz Processor, 2GB RAM, 80GB internal hard drive and a 500 GB external hard drive), A MacBook (Black) 2.4 GHz Processor, 2GB RAM, 250 GB internal hard drive, 2 Seagate 160GB pocket drives). I also own a Dell PC - 3 GHZ Pentium, 80GB and 300 GB internal hard drives, 4GB RAM. I use the M-Audio Firewire Solo on the Macs with Garage Band and Sonar 6 Producers Edition. The Dell has an M-Audio Delta 44 soundcard, and

Sonar 6 Producers Edition. All four machines work great, and I rarely have problems. I also use the Fender TBP-1 tube preamp and it sounds great. I use the M-Audio BX8a Monitors with a BX10s Subwoofer. I route sound to my speakers with the Presonus Central Station and protect my gear with 2 Furman power conditioners. The studio desk that I have is the Studio RTA Producers Station.

Mac or PC?

I prefer Mac. Macs are more user-friendly, they don't get viruses, and the support offered through the Apple Store is outstanding. The best feature is that by choosing a Mac now, you don't have to give up Windows, because this machine can run them both with Boot Camp, Parallels Desktop, or VMware Fusion installed. So you can still take advantage of software made for Windows but enjoy the superior quality, innovation, and lower learning curve of the Mac OS. Let me also say for the record that I don't have an endorsement relationship with Apple. I recommend them because they represent the simplest, most cost-effective, and user-friendly way to do the things I suggest in this book. I pay for my Mac stuff just like everyone else.

Why Did I Buy a PC?

I desperately love my Macs, but it's been frustrating over the years, paying a much higher price for Macs but not having access to some cool PC software. When I decided to write this book, there were two programs ("Writer's Blocks" and "StyleWriter") that I wanted to use, but they weren't available for the Mac. Those software developers didn't think we Mac users mattered, the Intel-based Macs were just a rumor, and I wanted to get started on this project, so I bought a Dell PC. Since it was newer and faster than my Mac G4, I decided to try Sonar 6 and the PC as my recording solution.

What Computer Do I Recommend?

I recommend one of the new Intel-based Macs. I've been waiting for over ten years for a single machine that could do everything, and it's finally arrived! These machines have everything you need to handle every aspect of your digital life as a musician. From recording (Garage Band), music library management (iTunes + iPod), to self-promotion and file sharing on the web (iWeb and .Mac), in print (Pages), on video (iMovie), and with multimedia (iMovie, iDVD). All of these are integrated programs and work well together. They're also easy to learn and use. I'll be talking more about them later when it's time to Equip Yourself, Educate Yourself, Make a Demo, and Self-Promote.

Other Stuff

Most of my income is from recording on projects at my home studio called "The Chase Lounge". I'm not a "gear-head" nor am I an engineer. I only know that good sound inspires me to play better, and my stuff sounds good to me. These days, a musician can get into home recording for less money than you might think. I do preproduction and drum programming with software like Sonar, Reason, Recycle, and Stylus RMX. None of my cables are anything special — they're just regular ol' cables. There's no sound dampening in my room, but I did add some extra insulation to the inner walls so my family wouldn't have to hear me working late at night. The only "special" features of my room are that I had a power line wired direct from my junction box to the room when I had the house built. I also had it decorated by an interior designer named Shinelia Little. All told, you could buy everything in my studio for about $6,000. If you were looking for the boutique list of gear, I'm sorry to let you down. But what can I say? The only live instrument that I cut at my place is electric bass, not orchestras, vocals, or drums. If I can get an excellent live sound from a bass rig that costs a little over $1,500, why should the gear that I record my bass with cost ten times that amount? And why should I buy enough gear to record an orchestra if I have no intent to do so? I'm a bass player, and my main job is to cut great bass tracks. Mission accomplished!

I know some gear-head musicians, professional engineers, and big studio owners who like to refer to "The Chase Lounge" as a joke. That's because many of them "hear" with their eyes and wallets. Brand names are important to them — *and* trying to keep up with the Joneses. They waste my time trying to debate with me about differences in gear or sound quality that only dogs can hear. But here's the reality from the bass chair — guys like me are killing them in the marketplace. Large amounts of expensive gear are not necessities anymore, because individuals are equipping their small project rooms well enough to record remotely. There are inexpensive pieces of gear that mimic the high-end stuff so well that you can't tell the difference on the final product. Using big fancy recording rooms is occurring less and less, because it's not always cost-effective to exclusively book them. The technology is so good that you don't have to spend the money for the seriously high-end computers anymore, because the low-end machines are also powerful, and excellent sound can be had with a few budget-priced audio interfaces on the market. The learning curves are also shrinking by the day, as companies are adding templates for everything from recording to mastering. Producers can hire me without leaving their preferred studios and without suffering a loss of recording or performance quality. In the five years that I've been recording my bass at my house, I've cut on eight top 10 singles (3 of them #1s) and nine top 10 CDs (4 of them #1s), a Grammy-winning tune, tons of TV and film dates, and I continue to enjoy a steady repeat business. I guess the joke's on me, right?

Some players criticize remote recording by talking about the merits of musicians recording together. I agree with them — but only to a point. I understand and enjoy the magic that happens when you have a room full of great players, but not all music needs that magic. Standard music beds for a local car dealership, for infomercials, or for porn are examples that come to mind. I'm just keeping it real.

So that's what's happening with the computer stuff. Now I'll move on to the musical instrument stuff. While there is some good advice in this next section, much of it is bass-specific. If you're not a bass player, but you're reading this section, I hope you can take some of these ideas and apply them to your own instrument. As I said before, these are my opinions, and I'm sure there are plenty of people who disagree with my views. I hope this book will inspire you to seek those people out, merge this information with their information, and come up with a solid viewpoint of your own. That said, I'll move on.

Common Sense and the Gear Head

When some people get serious about something, they become willing to spend tons of money on it. They want to feel satisfied that their tools are the best that money can buy and that they'll be able to conquer the world with them. Unfortunately, some mediocre players and gear heads believe great music is the result of the gear more so than the players. They'll hear a great tune and they'll say something ridiculous like, "That's sounds like a D411-x25 Compressor! The gold connectors and the 5819ArV40 crossover with a Gizmotic preamp make all the difference!" Pure BS.

Some mediocre players think that buying and using that "custom-made thingamajig equipped with the gadgetronic piezometer" will save them from having to work on their musical skills and give them a shot at being a virtuoso.

I give it up to experienced guys who know their gear and respect that they've formed their preferences, whatever they may be. But I also challenge any gear head to pick up any random CD and name all the gear used to make it. They couldn't do it, but they'd have you believe that a certain piece of gear can make or break your career. Don't fall for that! The truth is that music is subjective, and there's no scientific way to evaluate which music is better or worse. You can only decide if you like it or not. The same holds true for your gear — the only requirement is that it has to sound good to YOU and to the person paying you. Find and use the gear that inspires you to play your best, and then get on with making music!

It is true that the gear you buy is the backbone of your business, and solid decision-making can save time and money. You should also use some common sense when equipping yourself to be a Sideman. I dropped the ball on common sense when I was a Rookie Sideman, and I'll share the story with you so you won't make the same mistake.

Back in my Rookie Sideman days, I looked at what my favorite players were using, communicated with experienced owners, read reviews, considered my budget, and tested the gear myself before I dropped the cash on anything. I was thorough, but one day I slipped up and bought the "SuperCustom, Mel-Brown, Bass-Of-the-Gods".

This bass came with the newfangled-dangled electronics, 4 or 5 exotic woods with an oil-finished flame maple top, neck-thru construction, and cool fingerboard markings in mother-of-pearl. It took several months to build after I placed my order, but when it arrived it sounded great, and I couldn't wait to play it on the road! A few weeks later, I went on a short tour of some small towns in the Midwest.

The first few gigs were great, but one night the bass began to make a loud electronic crackling sound. I struggled through the rest of the performance and the next day took a cab to the local music store (30 miles away) hoping to find a repairman. I was in luck, and a highly recommended guitar repair man offered to look at my instrument. Apart from a few verbal jabs at my "SuperCustom, Mel-Brown, Bass-Of-the-Gods" having failed before it was a month old, he was cool and a big fan of custom instruments. I felt good until he removed the rear cover plate. The look on his face was one of horror, utter confusion, and dismay. He looked as if he'd seen a ghost, so I asked him what was wrong.

"I've never seen anything like this before," he replied. "In twenty-five years, I've worked on just about everything you could name, but I'm not familiar with these electronics at all. I'm sorry, but I can't help you."

I took a look for myself and felt doomed — it looked like a James Bond gadget inside! I started to panic, because my sound-check was in just two hours! Then I saw some other popular electronics that would work inside my bass. I had to pony up $300 for the electronics and a $50 fee to pull all of those fancy circuit boards out and install the new "Not-So-Super-Custom" electronics. To my surprise, the bass sounded just as good, but I'd spent most of the money that I was making that day.

When I returned home, I found that no one in Denver could repair the original electronics either. The builder said that I could ship the bass back to them at my own expense for "free" repairs but that they'd need it for at least two weeks because the "SuperCustom" electronics weren't in stock! Frustrated, I asked them what I should do in the meanwhile, and their response was, "Why don't we build you an identical bass so you have a spare!" Well, after that experience, and at $3,500 a pop, I wasn't too enthusiastic about buying another instrument from them.

Sometime later, I was in the studio with Chuck Loeb, and someone knocked the bass over while I was in the restroom. Something was very wrong after that, and the builder couldn't fix it. I finally sold the bass several months later and took a $900 loss. I used the money to buy two Fender Jazz Basses that I use to this day with no problems. I also had about $600 left over. Go figure!

The lessons that I learned are these:

Repairs & Maintenance

- I've had most of my problems with brand-new, fresh-on-the-market gear or custom gear — not old, used, or mass-produced gear. Strange but true. Your luck may be different, but before you buy any equipment, try to find the businesses in your area who can perform any necessary repairs or warranty work on that equipment. Program their phone numbers, e-mail addresses, and a contact name into your phone so you always have quick and easy access to them. Call them and find out how many repairs they've done on the gear you want. An excessive number of repairs should be a red flag. Another red flag is if you can't find a local business that has done repairs on the gear you want — your gear will be a learning experience for the repairer.

- It's a good idea to learn how to do some basic repairs on your own, because when your equipment does fail, *you* might be the only person within a hundred miles who cares. You should always anticipate making repairs at the most inconvenient times and under the worst circumstances. Trust me; it's not a matter of if it's going to happen — but *when*.

- "Custom" doesn't always mean better, so if you're going to go custom, try to balance your "custom wants" with "real-world use". When I spent $3,500 for the "SuperCustom, Mel-Brown, Bass-Of-the-Gods", I didn't really gain anything in terms of sound quality. Instead, I lost the ability to fix it myself or replace it quickly, and even worse, I dramatically reduced the number of people who could help me in an emergency.

Exit Strategy

Sometimes I just can't wait to get my hands on that new cutting-edge axe, gizmo, or doodad. The story I just shared with you is a perfect example of deciding to buy something and getting so excited that I never thought about the gear not working out. I'm referring to an exit strategy — a plan for whenever the gear doesn't work out. How would I deal with the "SuperCustom, Mel-Brown, Bass-Of-the-Gods" not working out? Would I sell it to a friend? Could I sell it on eBay? Should I sell it on consignment at the local music store? Will anyone else in the world want it — and will they buy it — even though it's built to my "SuperCustom Specs"? Will I be able to recover my investment? I didn't think about these questions before I bought it, but I guarantee that my choice would've been different if I had. I learned that rare, custom, or high-end gear is often expensive and inconvenient for maintenance, repair, and replacement.

When I experienced reliability problems, discovered some faults, and noticed a lack of capable repair shops, I became eager to get rid of the instrument. I learned that most buyers avoided buying the instrument from me for similar reasons, and I couldn't sell it for almost a year. Just remember my story before you drop some serious dough and then have to sell your gear to recover your investment.

Warranty and Insurance

I often buy a store's full replacement warranty with my expensive gear. That's because I always have some unusual event which makes my new gear become inoperable, get mangled, melted, soaking wet, stolen, etc. I don't advise buying the full replacement warranty on everything, but I've been able to take advantage of this coverage when my luck has turned bad. I learned a few things here too:

- Make sure you understand what your responsibilities are when making a warranty claim, because you may have to jump through so many hoops that it becomes pointless to make a claim on the coverage. The builder of my "SuperCustom, Mel-Brown, Bass-Of-the-Gods" wasn't going to charge me to replace the defective electronics or for the repair work, but I was going to have to pack, insure, and ship the instrument at my own expense, which was about $130. Not to mention that I was also going to be without the instrument for at least two weeks. And what if the same problems surfaced again — say three months later? It'd be the same deal — definitely not cool. Another negative was that the bass was hand-built. If there was ever a total loss, it would take several months to replace the instrument no matter what coverage I had — not good if my schedule was full. For me, the quality of a custom handmade instrument came nowhere close to offsetting the inconvenience of repairing or replacing it.

- Watch out for the flyer in the box with your new gear that says, 'If you have a problem, do not return this product to the store! Call 1-800-blah-blah-blah.' Don't buy that gear unless you have proof that their customer service is even worth bothering with.

A good rule of thumb is to buy as much of your gear as possible from reputable local stores that offer store warranties and have reasonable return policies. Insure or buy the extended full-service/replacement warranty for the expensive gear. Many insurance companies are wary of covering musical instruments for business use, but a great place to start looking for this insurance is to contact your local musicians union or to log on to

http://www.afm.org/public/home/index.php

You should also check out your homeowner's insurance or consider buying renter's insurance to cover your stuff if you don't own your home. My homeowner's insurance covers all of my gear in the event of theft or loss. I have to keep an accurate list of the serial numbers from each piece of gear, the receipt for its purchase, and its current market value. I keep such a list in PDF format, and I keep that list stored in my e-mail box so I can always retrieve it. You never know what, if, how, or when something can happen! Don't be paranoid, just stay ready!

Buying a Bass

Many beginning musicians or their parents ask me, "What's a good brand for a beginner?" Well, I can't help you if you're a teenager wanting to abuse your gear, spray-paint everything hot pink, or favor the instrument as an extension of your wardrobe. I can only tell you what's real and important here.

While it's true that there are many different instruments made by hundreds of companies, I believe there are five basic usable electric bass sounds that we have all come to know and love. They are:

1.　J - Bass (Fender Jazz Bass)
2.　P - Bass (Fender Precision Bass)
3.　Music Man Stingray (made by Ernie Ball but originally designed and introduced by Leo Fender)
4.　All of these models as five-string basses
5.　All of these basses as fretless models.

5-string basses with a low B have become the standard. Many people would argue that there are millions of different sounds, like 6, 7, 8, or even 9-string basses made with exotic woods or different combinations of electronics. I believe that the overwhelming majority of basses on the market are trying to mimic one of these five basic tones to some degree. If I were starting out today, I'd start with the Fender Jazz Bass V. You can't go wrong with the tone, and Fender instruments are fairly inexpensive, widely used and recognized, and have stood the test of time. There's a huge selection of third-party and aftermarket parts accessories, and just about anyone can maintain or fix one with only a little effort. Fenders also have a well-known and hard-earned reputation for allowing individuals to sound unique and find their own voice on the instrument, while providing a widely accepted tone. If you decide to get out of the music business, you can always sell a Fender and get most of your money back pretty quickly. The best feature of these instruments is that as long as you own one, you'll be able to use it. You don't have to take my word for this though. Listen to the best music of the 60s, 70s, 80s, and 90s up to now. More people play Fender Basses than anything else. I'd avoid the instruments which were made when CBS owned the company.

There are several companies who offer basses that are high quality copies of Fender designs. You should feel free to check them out. Note that higher-end basses are less common, less affordable, harder to sell, and it's likely you'll take a loss if you decide to get rid of it. Now don't get me wrong, I love the sound of Pensa Custom, Ken Smith, Sadowsky, Tobias, MTD, Sukop, Lakland, Mike Lull, Pedulla, and Fodera basses. I've owned, played, and recorded with all of them — I just don't recommend starting out with one. As your musicianship improves and your experience grows, you'll be able to decide whether to get into other vintage instruments, boutique models, more-string basses, or other specialty instruments. Guitarists, saxophonists, drummers, and keyboardists can apply this logic to buying their first instruments, too.

Active or Passive Electronics?

The answer to this question is subjective and depends on the player. Active electronics requires at least one 9-volt battery and offers the ability to fine-tune your sound with a set of controls on the bass itself. Passive electronics have less fine-tuning ability and don't need a battery. Some of today's most sought-after tones are on recordings from the 60s and 70s when passive pickups were all you could get. Around the mid-70s or so, Leo Fender introduced active electronics in his 'Music Man' basses which enjoyed popularity, in part because they offered new sound and new tone-shaping possibilities on the bass itself. The late 80s and early 90s brought an explosion in developing bass electronics, construction, and manufacturing.

Today, the technology is so good that active and passive electronics alike can deliver a great sound. The choices are many — I've had basses loaded with Bartolini, EMG, Aero, Fender, Lane Poor, Seymour Duncan, and other pickups, and even though they had their slight differences, they all sounded outstanding! I've had basses equipped with Sadowsky, Fodera, Bartolini, Fender, J-Retro, Aguilar, and other preamps in them, and guess what? Even though they had their slight differences, they all sounded outstanding! While in search of the "ultimate sound", I've toured, recorded, gigged, and practiced on basses built with all kinds of woods, pickups, and preamps. I've found all the best components to be only *slightly*, if at all, different than their competition.

My main considerations are the sound, the convenience, and whether I want to deal with batteries or not. Since these preferences are so subjective, the final decision should be yours and yours alone. If you choose to go with active electronics, you should check out this suggestion for all the bass manufacturers and their electronics makers:

Dear Sir:

As a Professional Bassist, I am grateful to the manufacturers for all the active electronics on the market. However, I wish all of you would put more consideration into what happens when your stuff doesn't work as it should. It's so annoying when the battery or some other component fails and the bass either stops making sounds or sends some loud electronic burp to my speakers. It's also really inconvenient having to use a screwdriver and having to expose all the delicate inner workings of my bass just to replace a battery. Please make it a standard practice to "build in" the ability for me to cover my ass onstage when your product fails. If your electronics need a battery or two, a pop-up battery compartment and a "get-out-of-trouble switch" should be standard. As a Professional Bassist, I need the ability to hit a switch and finish the song. Then, I need the ability to change the battery without tools and without leaving the stage before the next song starts.

Many of you have already addressed this, but several of you continue to ignore this issue, or you try to charge ridiculous extra fees for these features. Our craft and the state of the instruments that we use could benefit if these features were standard and didn't cost an extra $150 to $300. My son can hit a switch and change the frequency to get out of trouble while flying his $75 remote-controlled toy. He can also change the battery in the toy without any tools. Instrument makers should offer the same ability on all your instruments which cost hundreds more.

Sincerely,
Mel Brown

Ah! Now that I've gotten that off my chest, I'll move on. An important point to remember is that no one can tell what you're using on a mixed recording. They only hear if it's good or not. I heard a live Luther Vandross recording and thought that the sound of the bass was amazing. I thought that the bass had to be some high-end custom instrument. Then I bumped into the bassist on that CD, the talented and dirty, ol'-skool funky Byron Miller. He told me he used a cheap, Mexican-made version of a Fender Jazz Bass V. He'd replaced the pickups and added a preamp. After a total investment of $700, he was using the instrument to record along with one of the most important vocalists of our time!

I can tell you what I'm using in my own basses right now and why — but I remind you that this is one area where you have to get some hands-on experience and decide what you like the most.

Mel Brown's Basses

I own several instruments, so I'll just stick to the stuff I use now. I prefer J-style basses. My main recording bass is an all-stock Fender Jazz 5 with an 18-volt active preamp given to me by Rich McDonald at Fender. This was also my main live bass until recently. Next, I have a Fender Geddy Lee Jazz Bass 4 w/ J-Retro 01 given to me by Jay Piccurillo at Fender and two other stock Jazz basses I bought when I unloaded my custom-bass nightmare. I have a Fender P-Bass lying around with flat wound strings. Vintage tones are always popular and flat wounds can help you get a great retro sound. I also use a

Lakland DJ5 equipped with a J-Retro Deluxe and a pop-up battery compartment, a Pensa Custom J5, and a Tobias Classic 5. Except for the Tobias, they all have Fender or Aero single-coil pickups, and I'm installing J-Retro preamps with pop-up battery compartments in all of them. I like the J-Retro electronics because they offer great active and passive sounds at the flip of a switch, and they don't require any body modifications to install, but most of all — I like the sound. The J-retro will also continue to work without a battery, which has already come in handy.

I bought 4 Spectraflex cables about 10 years ago, and they still work so I still use them. I've used Dean Markley SR2000 strings exclusively for the last fifteen years, because I like how they feel and how they sound. If you'd like to hear me using all of this stuff, you can log on to www.melbrown.net and click on the link called "Spin Doctor". There, you will find some samples of recordings I've done with all the basses I've just described here. I also included info about which bass I've played on each project.

Buying an Amplifier

I recommend eventually having a few sizes of amplification systems — a small to medium — and a large or touring system. There are so many choices on the market today that you shouldn't look at my suggestions as gospel. I'm only offering you some information on where to start. Here's a breakdown of the systems by size:

Small to Medium-Size System

A good small-size rig should have at least one 10" or 12" speaker and be at least 100 watts. A good medium-sized rig should consist of a 2x10, 2x12, 1x15 combo amp or equivalent rated at no less than 200 to 400 Watts. The term 2x10 refers to the number of speakers in the cabinet (2) and the size of each speaker (10"). A small or medium-sized rig should be easy to carry or transport and should have all the features that large or touring-sized amps have — like a tuner output, XLR output, and effects loop. Having a small-size system is great for practicing and for gigs like churches, coffee shops, in the orchestra pit for a musical, or for rehearsing in someone's living room.

As I'm writing this chapter, I'm performing in the orchestra pit on a professional touring musical at Arizona State University. I'm using one of my small-size systems, a Fender Bassman rated at 100 watts with a single 10" speaker. The amp is working great and is more than enough for work in the pit and sending a good signal to the house. There's not much room in the pit, so the amps' small size and the fact that I can tilt it up toward my ears are great features. I have a slightly larger amp I use for these gigs, too. It's an Eden Nemesis with 2x10s rated at 200 watts. The amp is made of a lightweight composite material, and I've never found anything better for sound, power, and weight, so I keep it around.

Large-Arena Size System

A good large-size rig should consist of a rugged 4x10, 1x15 or equivalent speaker cabinet and a power amp or head rated at a minimum of 400 watts. Fender, SWR, Eden, Ampeg, Mesa Boogie, and Peavey all make some great 4x10 cabinets. They also make similar cabinets in other configurations and offer power amps or heads that fit into this category. Check them out, see what sounds good to you, and start from there. You'll use this rig for most of your larger live playing gigs around town. Another major consideration when choosing your large rig is loading it into your car, into the performance venue, and back home. I recommend buying a collapsible hand truck that will enable you to load in and out in one trip. I also recommend a hard case for the head and at least a soft cover for the cabinet. A great source of information about all the currently available gear is the Annual Buyers Guide from Miller Freeman. Do some research before you decide. My large rig right now is a Fender 800 Pro Head and a 4x10 cabinet. I'm waiting for the new Fender Pro 1200 Heads and a new 6x10 cabinet to be released soon.

The sky is the limit when it comes to your arena rig. You'll use this rig when you play at large places, like Madison Square Garden or Staples Center in LA. My arena rig is a Fender 800 Pro head and one Fender 8x10 Cabinet. It has tons of power, great tone, is reliable, and for me the best value for my money. I endorsed Eden Amplification for years and still like their gear, too. When I was touring, my main arena rig was all Eden - 800WT head, WT1000 power amp, two 4x10 cabs, and two 2x10 wedges. I've done side-by-side comparisons with my Eden rig against my Fender rig and I prefer the Fender because it has a foot switchable EQ (Equalization), a clean compressor, and a mute switch. The Fender stuff also costs a lot less. Most companies offer well-made systems that also sound great and come in various sizes. Check out as much as you can and see what works best for you. Don't ever buy any piece of gear that you haven't heard or tried out.

A Note About Speaker Cables

As a rule, I try to stay away from using quarter inch or banana cables to connect my speakers with my amplification. Speaker cables with Neutrik Speakon connectors are more durable, lock into place, and cannot be accidentally pulled out or vibrate free. Try to keep your cables as short as possible to avoid noise and accidental disconnections.

Buying a Tuner

I've read several opinions about whether a musician should use a tuner or not. Let me give you the final word on the subject. If you can accurately tune your instrument by ear, you should knock yourself out and do so at every opportunity. I'm good at tuning my bass by ear and do it when I'm in the mood. Now let's get real about tuning as it relates to show business. I'm talking about working the real world, in the trenches, and handling real gigs — not some "general principle" in some elitist Jazz head's classroom or clinic. The fact is you'd better own a tuner and have it in your gig bag, because in the real world, being in tune is a requirement 100% of the time. Receiving an opportunity to tune by ear before every show isn't. It's a fact that you're going to play more than a few gigs in terrible weather, noisy venues, and other bad circumstances. Nobody gives a crap how you get in tune at these gigs, but you'd better be in tune when it's show time. There have been countless occasions where I've had to wait for hours in the heat at some outdoor festival, then get onstage, and immediately play with no sound-check. While I was setting up, the music in the house PA was blaring, people were cheering, and promoters were schmoozing. The keyboard player was checking his sounds; the guitar player was checking his sounds, and the drummer was pounding his drums to get levels. I don't care who you are or who you *think* you are — you simply can't tune by ear in this environment! You'd better have a tuner and use it here, because if you're out of tune when Superstar X starts singing, you're out of a job. Here are some other gigs where a tuner literally saved my butt:

- I played a TV gig during December in New York City when the temperature was 30 degrees outside. Would you tune your bass and then leave it on a stand in that weather? I don't think so! Believe it when I say I pulled the bass out of the bag, the wood started contracting, and my tuning went straight down the tubes. With the cameras rolling, I had two minutes of having to be silent before playing a song on NBC for about 20 million viewers. Thank God for that tuner with the mute switch! If I hadn't had it, and Artist X noticed the bass was out of tune, I would've gotten dropped from that gig like a hot rock.

- I was onstage at Madison Square Garden filming a special for HBO in front of 19,000 screaming fans and a tech bumped my headstock on his way to fix the drums. I needed to check the tuning SILENTLY in the 20 seconds before the Artist started the next tune.

- I was in a session where the keyboard player, convinced that I was out of tune, continued to give me a hard time about it. His reputation was at stake and his ego was in the middle of what was becoming a heated exchange, so there was no reasoning with him. My tuner revealed that I was in tune and that he'd adjusted the tuning a few cents up on his keyboard but had forgotten. I guess we all make mistakes.

I have other true stories, but I'm sure you get the point. Expect the worst, but prepare to do your best. Tuners are tools that can help you do a better job in the real world. Buy one, put it in your gig bag, and USE IT!

Buying Effects

This is another area where individual taste takes precedence over everything else, but you should let the music tell you what pedals you need — or if you need any pedals at all. It doesn't make any sense to buy pedals that you're not going to use regularly, and I promise that lugging them around will quickly get old. The purpose of my pedal board is to provide all the sounds I need to play any music — including fretless, envelope filtered, acoustic Jazz, synthesizer-bass sounds, and good all-purpose tones. If you regularly use more than three pedals, I suggest getting them organized or trying multi-effects units to see if you can consolidate without sacrificing tone. Cases made by Boss, SKB, Fuhrman, and others provide solutions for leaving your pedal arrangement intact — which can save you valuable set-up and tear-down time. If you're using multiple pedals, I suggest adding a volume pedal to compensate for differences in output, and keep a spare of any pedals which you use extensively.

For cables, check out George L's. You can make them yourself to any length that you need, which helps keep your pedal board clean and professional looking. George L's also gives you a solid solution to test and repair your cables at the gig if you have to. As with any equipment, read your manuals and find out how the manufacturer recommends using a piece of gear, then adapt their information to your own situation. Don't ever try any new equipment while on your gig — always try it out at home on your own time first. Dial your sounds up at home and troubleshoot any problems. You'll be glad you did. Here's a brief description of the pedals I use and why. I'll also be posting samples of my sounds at www.fromzerotosideman.com. I hope this gives you some direction and a place to start.

Digitech BP50, 80, 200 Multi-Effects Unit

I use this pedal for Reverb, Chorus, and Octaver sounds, but the main reason that I use it is for the fretless sound it has. There was a time when I had to cop a lot of Pino Palladino's bass lines — back when he played the fretless bass with an octaver. I didn't feel like lugging my fretless to the gigs for 2 or 3 songs, and this unit helped me cop it exactly. I don't have to cop Pino's lines anymore, but I've gotten good at mimicking a fretless, so I always have it in case someone asks me to bring a fretless or for cover tunes. Between my left hand articulation and this unit, you can't tell the difference between my wanna-be-a-fretless-or-acoustic bass and a real one.

EBS Bass IQ

Besides the obvious envelope-filtered grooves and required Bootsy Collins funk sounds, I use this pedal to create a soulful soloing voice. I like copying vocalists or the Moog synthesizer when I blow solos or play the heads to R & B tunes. You can check out this sound on my YouTube page – www.youtube.com/chaseme40. Click on the tune called "Be With You" or on "Joe's Sample".

Akai SB1 Synth Bass Pedal

When Akai stopped making this pedal, I thought it was one of the worst decisions that I'd ever seen a big company make. This pedal, with an EQ pedal, removed the need for me to play a keyboard bass! I use this pedal by itself to cop all the old-school keyboard bass sounds on tunes by the SOS Band, Carl Carlton, The Gap Band, Prince, Chaka Khan, The Isley Brothers, Zapp & Roger, etc. But if I add an EQ pedal, I can cop the new Moog-like sounds used by 50 Cent, Usher, Ne-Yo, T-Pain, SWV, Mario, Timbaaland, and more. To this day, the sound of this pedal and the Bass IQ causes the most questions from other bassists! They walk up and say, "Now... what are you using to get that keyboard sound?" I used this pedal on a top ten single called "Throwin' it Down" on Wayman Tisdale's CD called "Rebound".

Boss Bass EQ (3)

I like to EQ every sound I use separately. As a bassist, the difference between a good sound and a great sound is the right EQ, and I recommend checking it out if you want to handle your business as a Sideman. I used to dial up a single EQ setting on the amp and try to use it for everything, but I disliked some of my sounds because there was always something that I wanted to adjust. To explain my point, here are two of the sounds I use and how I roughly EQ them:

- Slapping – My slap sound has the lows and highs boosted, and the midrange cut at 700 or so.

- Finger-Style – My finger-style sound is flat with a slight boost from the 250s to 700s.

The problem here is that I switch from slapping to finger-style playing a lot. If I used my finger-style EQ for everything, my finger-style grooves would sound great, but my slap sound would include the midrange that doesn't sound good to me. If I used my slap EQ for everything, my slap sound would be great, but my finger-style grooves would be boomy or muddy and lack clarity. In other words, the characteristics of a good slap sound for me are exactly the opposite of those of a good finger-style sound, and I need them both to be perfect when I use them. My Boss EQs give me that ability. The only problem that I have with these pedals is that I can only have one setting for each unit. Boss makes another pedal called the EQ-20 that allows you to save 9 settings in a single box. The EQ-20 doesn't work for me because the layout of the controls requires me to bend over and push a button to select which EQ I'm using. Since I often switch EQ settings during a song, it's inconvenient and impractical. I wish Boss had made the EQ-20 so one of the footswitches controlled the ON or BYPASS function and the other scrolled through the user saved EQ settings.

Boss LS-2 Line Selectors (3)

When I'm not using my effects, I don't like my signal running through several boxes even though they may be in BYPASS mode. The three LS-2s allow me to remove the effects from my signal chain until I need them, and they also allow me to adjust the output levels of my various effects with a volume control for each loop. I think this goes a long way toward keeping my rig as quiet and balanced as much as possible, and it also allows me to get to a combination of pedals with one step.

And there you have it. After you get your gear together, it will be time to get music on the brain and Educate Yourself. Let's move on.

EDUCATE YOURSELF

The Theory of Music

When I started learning music theory back in high school, the amount of information was overwhelming — and discouraging. It just seemed impossible to learn it all, so I relied on memorizing the songs I had to play. One cool thing about listening to the recordings was that everything I needed to know in order to perform the tune authentically was right there. Much of this information was unavailable in the written music. Features such as feel, sound, note choices, articulation of the notes, all of which I mimicked, were absent on the sheet music. This gave me an advantage, because the students relying solely on the sheet music missed this information, and their playing often lacked the style and character of the recordings. For me, this highlighted the value of learning music by ear. After I learned the song by ear, my music teacher would teach me the terminology to describe what I was hearing on the recording, what I was playing on my bass, and what I was seeing on the lead sheet. It wasn't long before I noticed musical similarities and started transferring information between songs. That's when I realized that the purpose of music theory is to describe musical sounds with names and words. Describing music with names and words offers a pathway to teach, analyze, and communicate about music without having to play it on an instrument.

I started looking at every song as having two sides — a Technical Side and a Stylistic Side.

The Technical Side has to do with recognizing and having an understanding of the basic musical building blocks used to compose the song and correctly performing them on my instrument. By "Musical Building Blocks", I mean the key signature, time signature, chords, tempo, note choices, rest choices, melodies, harmonies, and so on. The correct execution on a particular instrument is the priority here. Being able to read, speak, or understand these mechanics in a way other than hearing and playing them is a plus but not mandatory.

The Stylistic Side has to do with the distinct musical vocabularies, sounds, and performance traditions that suggest a song's category. Music serves an important social purpose to people of many different ethnicities, and *authenticity* is everything. Mastering a category requires listening to, learning, and being able to mimic literally hundreds of songs within that category. To sound good, you've got to bring the Technical and Stylistic sides together whenever you play any song.

Why? Because songs are what make the world go 'round in the music industry. They are the individual "units" of music sold in stores, on iTunes, being broadcast by radio, sung by singers, and used for music videos. Learning and playing songs is your core business as a Sideman. As such, sounding bad on songs can damage your reputation and hurt your chances of succeeding.

Most musicians know that they sound the best on songs they know and love, but they advertise that they play "all styles". Some of them really think they can play "all styles" until they find out the hard way that they can't. I've seen some "all styles" players crash and burn. I've seen Head Bangers struggling to play Motown songs, Funkateers struggling with Country songs, and Jazzers taking a dump on simple Pop songs. This happens because those players fail to bring the two sides together, or they make the mistake of dismissing the stylistic side of the song as unimportant. They are also unaware that the songs they know largely determines who they are as players. You can avoid this pitfall by knowing who you are as a player. Here's how: Grab a piece of paper and divide it into three columns.

1. In the first column, write the name of all the songs you love listening to the most and can play from memory with no help.

2. In the second column, write the genre of each song.

3. In the third column, write the name of the Artist for each song.

You can also do this exercise by making a play list in iTunes. When you're done, add up the total number of tunes in each genre.

The genre with the most songs is who you are now as a player. The other genres are you also — but not as much. If your list has one hundred Rock songs, eighteen R&B songs, and only five Country songs, Congratulations, you're a Rocker. Don't take that four-hour Country gig next week. You got a call today for a Jazz gig? I wouldn't do it if I were you!

You should use the top three or four Artists' names that appear in the third column to describe your style: "I'm a Rock player in the style of Kiss, Incubus, Linkin Park, Judas Priest, and Def Leppard."

I do declare! So that's why you went down in flames when you had to play "Material Girl" at that wedding last week!

Now make a list of twenty other players who you admire and at least twenty songs that they play on, including their genre. Again, add up the total songs for each genre. The genre with the most songs is who you want to be. Compare your lists and you'll get a clear picture of what you're doing right and the areas that you need to address. Once you have a handle on who you are and who you want to be, you'll need to make a major musical decision:

Do I Continue To Play By Ear, Or Do I Learn To Read Music?

Reading sheet music falls on the Technical Side of playing songs. Even though there are two sides to every song, those sides are not necessarily equal. In the real world, the most important element is bringing authenticity (Stylistic Side) to the music at hand, and that can only come from learning by ear. You don't have to be able to read music or graduate from music school to be successful, but being a Sideman is a small service-oriented business, remember? If you want to work as much as possible, you need to be comfortable working with musicians who read music *and* with those who only play by ear. More importantly, you should be able to make music readers *and* nonreaders comfortable working with **you.** Reading music will open doors to many opportunities not offered to nonreaders. If you aspire to be in the studios playing other peoples' songs — you should read. If you want to be a candidate for that last-minute call from Unfamiliar-But-Very-Important Person K or Speven Steilberg — you should become a reader. If you choose to learn, I recommend private instructions to learn basic notation, harmony, and technique. As a bassist, I'd buy the following books and use them at the lessons:

- *Hal Leonard, Electric Bass Book*, by Ed Friedland, Volumes 1, 2, and 3

- *Inside Improvisation,* by Jerry Bergonzi, Volumes 1, 2, and 3

- *How to Play Bebop,* by David Baker, Volumes 1, 2, and 3

- *Patterns For Jazz*, by Jerry Coker

- *The Jazz Sound*, by Dan Haerle

- *The Working Bassist's Toolkit*, by Ed Friedland

- *Super Sight-Reading Secrets*, by Howard Richmond

- *Slap Bass DVD,* produced by Ed Friedland

- *Nothing but the Blues*, by Jamie Aebersold

- *The Jazz Theory Book,* by Mark Levine

- *The Augmented Scale in Jazz,* by Walt Weiskopf

- *Coltrane: A Player's Guide To His Harmony,* by Walt Weiskopf

- *Intervallic Improvisation*, by Walt Weiskopf

- *The True Cuban Bass*, by Carlos Del Puerto & Silvio Vergara

- *The Latin Bass Book*, by Oscar Stagnaro

- *Modern Reading Text in 4/4 Time,* by Louis Bellson (Get the odd time book too!)

Learning to read music is going to improve your ability to learn songs quickly and will also strengthen your ability to play by ear. The books that I mentioned above will give you a rock-solid foundation in the basics. If you're interested in more information, check out www.aebersold.com. They have books on just about any topic that you can imagine about musical knowledge and performance. The Internet itself is available 24 hours a day, 7 days a week, all year long. It's also a treasure trove of free information, videos, transcriptions, and lessons. I can't encourage you enough to take advantage of the Internet to supplement your learning.

Regardless of your decision about whether to learn to read music or not, it's time to get moving on learning songs. I'm confident that the books listed above will contain most of what you'll need to know to become *technically* competent as a player, but they're only half of what you'll need to be **musically** competent as a player. You're going to need to know and be able to play a lot of songs authentically to survive as a Sideman in any city. But where do you start? Which songs should you learn first? Read on...

Start Learning Songs!

Learn the songs that will get you into the local scene and working as soon as possible. When I was starting out, I noticed that bandleaders would hire someone who "knew the songs" before they hired "a great musician" almost every time. So I decided that the logical first step was to make a "Master List" of the songs that the Sidemen in town were playing for money. I got recordings of those songs and learned every one of them. I figured that if I knew all the songs, I'd eventually be an eligible candidate to do all the gigs. I was right. I can tell you with complete confidence; the more songs you know, and the better you play them, the more you will work, period.

Here's How You Put Your Own "Master Song List" Together:

1. Make a list of all the working bands and General Business bandleaders in your area who play the style of songs you're

good at now and want to become good at over time. You can find the bands in your area in the entertainment section of the local newspaper or in the free weekly newspapers that advertise local restaurants and entertainment. These free papers exist in a lot of cities, the *Village Voice* in New York, the *LA Weekly* in Los Angeles, or the *New Times* in Phoenix. As for me, I planned to hear all the working bands that played Jazz, Smooth Jazz, R&B, Dance, Rock, and Country. I wasn't into Punk, Heavy Metal, Gothic, or joining original bands who were "trying to make it" so I didn't waste any time with them. Or you can just ask any musician or music teacher where to find live music in your town. If you're planning to move to a new city, you may want to plan a trip to do some research in the city you're moving to. If taking the trip is not an option, try to get the free paper from that city, and then use the Internet and e-mail as much as possible to find out what songs the bands are playing there. You'll find that many bands provide a list of songs they perform and even have some MP3 samples on their web sites.

2. Go and see each band perform. Bring a notebook stocked with paper and make an accurate list of the songs they play. If you have a small recording unit, bring it along but be discreet while using it. Don't be a jerk by giving out or selling your recordings either. Try to find out the original Artists names for any original and unknown songs. After you see a few bands, you'll find that they all perform many of the same songs.

3. You should also watch and make notes of other important aspects of the performance. Examples are, how the people dress, what gear they're using, who is the person in charge, performance times, and the number of and the length of breaks. Part of your education is learning how to use different pieces of gear. If you see a guy using an SWR setup, you should stop by Guitar Center with your bass and learn how that gear works. Learn how to dial up a sound as close to your own as possible, and practice playing with another player's settings, because they may not let you change them when you sit in. You'll put all this information to good use later.

4. Get as many recordings of the songs on your list as possible. Organize your songs by genre on your Master List, and keep a separate play list of each band's songs under that band's name. This is where your computer, iTunes, an iPod, and the Internet can help you.

5. Start learning! You should learn the original versions, and try to remember how each band performed each tune and incorporate all of this knowledge into your playing. Nonreaders will have to commit all of this music to memory. Reading players can look on the Internet for sheet music or transcribe the songs themselves. Always make a chart of any song you learn. I did this for several reasons:

- It would save me from having to learn any song twice from scratch and help me get through the gig if I forgot something in the song.

- It forced me to improve my reading skills, my transcribing skills, my knowledge of song forms, my musical penmanship, etc. I'd compare the charts that I wrote to charts known to be accurate and correct myself as necessary. This was a painfully slow process at the beginning, but over the years I've become proficient and very fast at it. That's not to say that I wasn't open to using preexisting charts to learn songs in the beginning. I bought the new legal "Real Books" and "Fake Books" and used them to speed up my learning.

- It provided proof to bandleaders that I'd taken the time to learn their material. This displayed my seriousness and commitment to my craft, and it made them a lot more open to allowing me to "sit in". "Sitting in" is a method of self-promotion that I'll talk about in the next chapter.

6. Visit each band's performances regularly, and make note of how their live performances of songs differs from the original versions. Learn these differences as if you had already been

hired to perform with these bands. You should see each band perform at least five times to get a clear picture of what's happening musically and socially on the gig. On your third or fourth visit, introduce yourself to the bandleader and the band. They've seen you before, and they'll probably be cool about sharing information with you about the gig and other players they work with. Ask them if they know of any more bands who play similar songs, and, if so, where and when they play. Plan to see them and add their songs to your Master List.

If you're a reader and studying with a teacher, you should have a long list of questions for them to answer while you're learning all of these songs. Hopefully, your teacher can answer all of your questions or direct you to someone who can. I didn't have a teacher, so I let the songs determine my practice regimen and the performance standard I wanted to achieve.

What About Tablature?

Please note that when I say you should become a reader I don't mean being able to read tablature. Tablature (or "Tab" as it's affectionately known") has been around in various forms for centuries. These days, tab can be a helpful tool mostly when learning songs by ear and a recording of the song is available. If you like Tab and it's available feel free to use it. (Remember, for a non-reading gig, no one really cares how you learn songs, they only care that you can play them authentically at the show.) If you don't have a recording of a particular tune Tab won't help you very much because it lacks rhythmic and timing information. Log on to the internet and find some Tab for a song you've never heard. Then make a recording of yourself playing what you think that Tab specifies.When you're done, log on to iTunes, buy the song and listen to how the song really goes. 'Nuff said...

What About Practicing Technique?

I took the same "learn songs" approach to working on technique. For example, instead of making a random decision to work on slapping, I learned songs that required me to be a "fluent slapper" such as:

- "Run For Cover" and "Hideaway" – Live Versions – (David Sanborn)

- "Forget Me Nots" (Patrice Rushen)

- "Glide" (Pleasure)

- "Pessimisticism" (Crusaders)

- "Love Zone" (Billy Ocean)

- "Jump To It" (Aretha Franklin)

- "Stomp" (Brothers Johnson)

- "Let's Work" (Prince)

- "Love You Anyway" (Cameo)

- "Never Too Much" (Luther Vandross)

- "Same Ol' Love" (Anita Baker)

- "Paradise" (Change)

- "99" (Toto)

- "You Can't Get What You Want" (Joe Jackson)

- "Bottoms Up" (Victor Bailey)

I had to improve my slap bass playing to perform these songs live. I did so by learning how to play each song slowly and then gradually increasing the tempo until I could play them significantly faster than the original versions. I also made a "slap bass workout" CD (you can make a playlist in iTunes now) that had all these slap songs back to back to practice with. I also collected slap exercises from everywhere and used them to practice. These days, you can buy inexpensive portable devices that will play songs slowly but still preserve the pitch and allow you to plug your instrument in and play along, like the 'Bass Trainer' from Tascam.

Now that you've got your musical skills together, a solid repertoire, and some knowledge about who's working in town, it's time to introduce yourself to the scene. It's time to make a demo.

MAKE A DEMO

What is a Demo?

"Demo" is short for demonstration. In the music industry, a demo is a short but organized presentation intended to introduce you, to show others what you can do, and to create work opportunities. To include multimedia on demos is the new standard, and it's never been easier to produce. These days, the home computer, CDs, and the Internet make producing a multimedia demo as easy as 1-2-3. CDs are excellent for placing information directly into the hands of specific people, while the Internet provides a convenient, inexpensive solution for delivering information to the rest of the world. The software industry has also come a long way in reducing the price and reducing the steep learning curves previously associated with production and delivery of multimedia.

Why Make a Demo?

You want to make a demo because no reasonable person trusts a stranger. We don't invite strangers into our homes or let our children speak to them. Most of us view strangers as potentially threatening ("Stranger Danger"), and we reduce our potential risk by keeping them in the "Stranger Zone". Think about the last time you came across a stranger. I'll bet most of your thoughts about that person were negative until you had good reason to change your mind. This truth carries over into our business activities. No one wants to deal with a stranger, let alone hire one. A demo offers an opportunity for folks to check you out at their own convenience, without risk, and at a safe distance. By answering most of the common questions people ask, my demo quickly gets me out of the "Stranger Zone" and into the "I'm Going to Call Mel Brown for Some Fat and Tasty Groovin' Bass Zone." Although there are a million variations to these questions, they are all based on a small few, such as:

- Who are you?
- Where are you from? (What's your family status, kids, and what brought you to town?)
- What instrument do you play?
- What style of music do you play?
- Have you ever played any [enter style here]?
- Can you play [enter style here]?
- Can you read music — if "yes" how well?
- Who have you worked with?
- Do you have any references?
- How old are you?
- Where and when can I hear you?

- How easy are you to work with?

- What do you look like?

- Do you have a web site, MySpace, or YouTube page?

- What are your rates for [enter work type here]?

Another benefit of having a demo is that it reduces the need for you to talk extensively about yourself to others or to make a "hard sell" of your service. A lot of musicians are turned off by newbies trying to talk their way into a gig, so having a good demo can be a real plus. Musicians are like a bunch of nosy old women — they don't want you to know they are curious and are watching other players, but they always are. Players might be dismissive when you hand them your demo, but even if it takes awhile, most of them will eventually check you out, because they want to see if you suck! And then they'll talk about you to their friends!

How Do I Put My Demo Together?

I use two ingredients to make a demo that will introduce and educate others about me. The first ingredient is information about me and includes five elements:

1. A Biography
2. A Selected Discography
3. Some Word of Mouth
4. Some Press
5. Endorsement Examples

The second ingredient is the mechanism/devices used to deliver the information about me to others. I'll explain both ingredients in-depth so you understand.

Ingredient #1: Information About Me

As I said, this ingredient is made of five elements:

Element 1: Biographical Information

My biography is a condensed account of my career — from its beginning to the present. I mainly include the high points — such as awards and important accomplishments, but I also share a little history as far back as high school. I produce my bio in several formats to maximize access to the information. The goal here is to make someone feel good about taking me out of the stranger zone.

Text Bio

I have two text biographies that I'm using right now. The first is a longer history written in the first person. Even though it's text, I try to show my personality by keeping it real and by using a lighthearted and upbeat writing style. (I recommend writing in a style that matches your personality.) This longer biography is for anyone interested in hiring or recommending me and who is seeking as much information as possible. You can see my text bio on my website here:

http://www.melbrown.net/mel-who.php

PDF Bio

This is a three page downloadable version of a short text biography. It contains a brief introduction written in the third person, a Discography, Performances, and a TV and Film page. I use PDF documents to insure that they look exactly as I intend when printed by the end user. I use a template in the program called 'Pages' on my Mac to create it. The PDF is for the users who still live in an "analog" world, and it can be faxed if necessary. You can download my PDF bio from my web site here:

http://www.melbrown.net/MelWho.pdf

Video Bio (a.k.a. "EPK" or "Electronic Press Kit")

This is the most important item in my self-promotion and continues to be the most effective. This is a version of my bio that uses video and a sound track to communicate information. It's similar to a text bio in that it's a condensed account of my career, but I can highlight information with pictures and video footage. I studied TV shows such as *Entertainment Tonight*, local news, and especially VH1's *Behind the Music* to get an idea of how to tell a good five minute story. I start by gathering all of my up-close video clips of me doing my thing and place them in the timeline in iMovie. The clips are in no particular order, and I start by reading my text bios while they play. First, I get rid of any clips that don't look good. Next, I'll change some of the words to fit what's on the screen, or I'll adjust the video by slowing it down or changing the order of my clips. I learned that TV shows rarely use fancy transitions between shots, so I use them sparingly.

Eventually, I have a solid combination of narration and footage. I record the narration into Garage Band, add it to my video, and edit as necessary or add background music. I hate the sound of my own speaking voice, so once I like the overall presentation, I hire a professional voice-over person to record the final version using my script. Local radio personalities are a great choice, and sometimes they can do the recording at their station, which always sounds great. I used a local smooth-Jazz DJ called Michael Kay on mine. When it's finished, I save my video for delivery on my web site, on Enhanced CD-ROM, DVD, and as a downloadable video for iPhone (or other "smart" cell phones), iPod, MySpace, and YouTube. iMovie makes this a no-brainer because it optimizes your video for these outlets with one click.

When I edited my first video bio back in '97, I wanted to use some still photos, but they were anticlimactic because they didn't move like the rest of the video. Then I noticed how the still pictures were moving on *Behind the Music*. By slowly panning in, panning out, or from side-to-side, their still pictures were as effective as the video footage. I learned that this effect is called the "Ken Burns Effect". Another effect that I wanted to use was moving text on the screen with my video, like in the title shot for *Behind the Music*. I wanted to use these techniques for my video bio but I didn't know how, didn't have the equipment, and there was no program available that I could quickly employ to do it. I called around Denver, and the folks doing video stuff in town were just too expensive. These effects and some others come with iMovie. They're easy to learn and use.

With reality TV being so popular right now, the quality of the video doesn't even have to be that good to make a good impression. If you're willing to put some time and effort into it, the results can be spectacular. I recommend that you check out what's possible. If you do an impressive video, other people will try to impress their friends by showing them your video and so on, and so on, and so on. This happened when I moved to LA, and it was a huge help in getting my name around. You can see my video bio here:

http://www.melbrown.net/mel-video.php

Audio Bio

My audio bio serves as my standard demo. This is what people hear when they put my Profile into their car or home stereos. I edit short audio clips of my work together in Garage Band so my skills as a player are on display. These clips may be from CD projects, live shows, audio portions of video performances, or items that I record specifically for the demo. Bass solos are rare in the Pop-music world, but strong musicianship is always a plus. I use recorded solos to showcase my ability to navigate changes and to demonstrate my technical abilities on the bass. For those users who don't have access to a computer, I go the extra mile with my audio demo by including recorded clips from some of my previous clients and the audio track from my video biography.

Element 2: Selected Discography and Styles

Documenting my recording experience has always resulted in more session work. I use text and multimedia materials to communicate this information. Rather than presenting every project, I choose a few that collectively paint the best picture of me as a player. I use the text version of my discography in my PDF bio. For multimedia, I scan CD covers into iPhoto, and import the songs that I'd like to edit into Garage Band. I trim each tune down to be about a minute or two. Then I bring them back into iTunes and convert them to MP3s for the web and to AAC for inclusion into my multimedia Profile Presentation. I also try to include a Word-of-Mouth clip from each Artist represented. Using multimedia here can be helpful, because a potential client may not be familiar with the Artists you've worked with — and mentioning an unfamiliar Artist's name as your biggest accomplishment can have a negative effect. Remember what I said about famous and struggling musicians? Unfamiliar Artists are almost always assumed to be struggling. By using pictures and sound, folks are able to see and hear the quality of the work and form an educated opinion.

I include the section called "Styles" to highlight anything lacking in my discography. A corporate bandleader or someone who runs a cover band may be curious about my ability to play certain styles or songs needed for their gigs. I take a look at my "Master List" of songs and add several songs commonly played in most of the working bands in town to address these concerns. If I'm still lacking anything, I'll pick some songs from each specific genre and add them. You can see my discography here:

http://www.melbrown.net/spin-doctor.php?albid=1

Element 3: Word-of-Mouth Clips

When I work for clients, I ask them to record a statement about the experience. They're usually happy to do it, and I'll use a mini-disc recorder for the voice and my camera phone to get a picture. Some Artists will suggest a picture from their own web site. Other times I'll use a video camera to capture their comments. After I record the statement from the Artist or client, I'll bring it into iMovie or iTunes at the highest possible quality. I can separate the audio from the video clips in iMovie for use in the audio bio if necessary. I think that if folks can get it "straight from the horse's mouth" they won't need to ask around, and I'll get hired sooner.

Everyone relies on traditional word of mouth to a degree, and it's a powerful form of advertising. Word of mouth has its flaws, too. First, word of mouth is someone's opinion, and that opinion is affected by the source's musical ability, emotional state, personality, beliefs, social status, and so on. In other words, people can change their word of mouth to be positive or negative at their own discretion. Also, the source of the word of mouth may be simply passing on third or fourth-hand information and may not actually know the person being discussed. This makes some comments unverifiable, unreliable, and occasionally a liability.

Second, word of mouth can be slow. Musicians may take their sweet time to ask around about you. Or your positive word of mouth could be delayed because of an act of God. I'll give you an example. Assume that my friend Victor Wooten and I are unknown bass players trying to make it in LA. We both show up at the same club to sit in and to hopefully incite some positive word of mouth for ourselves. I sit in first, play well, and even blow a killer solo. Then Vic pulls the Atomic Thumb out of his pocket and proceeds to destroy the joint, does a back flip, and finishes by magically appearing on the roof of the building. I guarantee you that most of the word of mouth will be about Vic for a while! Folks will have to recover from this before I can expect them to begin spreading some positive word of mouth about me — if they ever do at all! I try to minimize my reliance on others by supplying my own authentic word of mouth. You can check out my word-of-mouth clips here:

http://www.melbrown.net/word-of-mouth.php?wid=3

Element 4: Press

Being featured in a magazine or other publication is a great honor and can go a long way toward strengthening your reputation. I scan covers of the publications into iPhoto and then present the text of the article as it originally appeared. Again, even if the end user is unfamiliar with publication, here they can come away with a better impression of your accomplishment. You can see my press here:

http://www.melbrown.net/scribes.php?scid=2

Element 5: Endorsement Information

I include this information as a benefit to the companies investing in my career. I check out their advertising and try to do similar ads featuring me instead of 'That Famous Guy' they use. This often leads to the company using my photos in their promotions, thus increasing my own visibility and market value. Here I scan the photos into iPhoto, borrow text from the manufacturers web site, and supplement it with my own text. You can see an example on my web site here:

http://www.melbrown.net/endorsements.php?endid=3

Ingredient #2: Delivery Mechanism/Devices

After I produce all the information about me, I organize it into presentations that others can view.

Enhanced CD

My main demo is an Enhanced CD that I call a Profile. Except for the World Wide Web, this device guarantees the most information being seen, heard, used, and shared by the most people. It may seem like a lot of work, but if you have a web site, you've essentially done the hardest part of putting a demo like this together. When I meet a potential client, I don't want to rely on them to go to my web site or MySpace page later, nor do I want to just hand them a business card. I want to put everything they need to know about me into their hands right then. I use technology to make it simple and convenient for them to check me out ASAP — because the sooner they see me do my thing, the sooner they'll call me for work. Enhanced CDs are the perfect self-promoting tool for musicians because they're capable of three functions:

- It can connect a user to my web site — since a CD can't be updated once it's burned, this is an important feature. I include all the standard information that will never change on the CD and then program the disc to connect with a web page that can deliver updated information.

- It plays like any other regular CD — this is great because there are still people who don't own or use computers. These folks can use their car or home stereo to listen to my demo. No need to get cute with the small business card size CDs — because you can't play those in the car.

- It can carry an interactive presentation that's similar to my web site — and is compatible with Mac and Windows computers. I'm able to showcase myself without an Internet connection or its limits. I use a $79 program called MediaWorks to make the presentation interactive by adding buttons, sound effects, and navigation. It's easy to use and also contains a suite of tools to capture and edit video, audio, photos, build graphics, and add animation. Their web site has several great tutorials, and the customer support is excellent. If you'd like to see my latest demo, you can e-mail me and I'll send it to you. You can check out MediaWorks here:

http://www.mediaworkssoftware.com/

iPods

iPods are the new Rolodex for the music industry because they're an excellent delivery medium for the video and song clips in your multimedia demo. I include a folder on my demo that an end user can drag into iTunes. The end user can make a playlist under my name, and add my audio clips and video to it. I also make these materials downloadable from my website, MySpace, and YouTube pages. I also keep playlists of other players on my own iPod to remind me who I should hire or recommend for work.

Cell Phones

Like iPods, cell phones are a massive opportunity for musicians who self-promote. While trying to compete with the wildly successful iPod, cell phone manufacturers have redesigned their products to simultaneously work as phones, web portals and universal media players. Cellular service providers are seeking to increase their profits by using their networks to market, sell and deliver video entertainment, music, and web surfing direct to their subscribers' phones. I think it's safe to say that over the next few years this will increasingly become the standard. Any self-promoting Sideman can benefit enormously by their efforts because now almost anyone can present a video audition on any cell phone!

When it comes to phones these days, the choices are many. Some modern cell phones (like the iPhone, Instinct, Treo and Blackberry) are the equivalent of some desktop computers and enable users to

- surf the internet,
- buy, download, and play high quality music and TV shows,
- record, display, and send video or pictures,
- wirelessly send contact information,
- check, compose, and send e-mail,
- organize contacts,
- send text messages

The bad news is some of these machines are expensive. The good news is you have several other choices to put this power in your pocket because most budget priced cell phones have similar abilities. The best news is that you'll struggle to find a single person not carrying a cell phone. Since I use video to self-promote, I decided to explore the possibility of delivering my video bio on cell phones.

With any technology, you first learn that it's not perfect. Next, you learn is that most people are notoriously behind in learning and using it – and resistant to doing so. I'll give you an example:

Back in the day when a new contact asked for my phone number, I was happy to give the number but grew frustrated as that person fumbled through entering my name into their phone. Many times they'd get certain information wrong, then give up and say something like "I'll just get your e-mail address and all that stuff later." I'd rarely hear from them, and learned from experience that most people never follow through. The combination of them not knowing how to use their phone, inaccurate information and lack of follow through added up to wasted time and missed opportunities for me. I need all of my new contacts to have accurate information to find, audition, and contact me, and recommend me to others if they feel so inclined. Then I found out about Bluetooth technology. Since most cell phones have a "<Send contact via Bluetooth>" feature, I thought I could enter my name, number, e-mail address, and website URL in the address book of my phone, and store a video introducing myself too. When someone requested my number, I'd use Bluetooth to send my info and video directly to my new contacts' phone. Problem solved! I wanted to test my idea, so I spent a few days at retail outlets for AT&T, Sprint, T-Mobile, and Verizon Wireless trying and learning about Bluetooth. Well, remember what I said about technology not being perfect? I tried to send my contact information and video via Bluetooth to every phone that was on display at each of the stores. Here's what happened:

- All the phones successfully received the name and number, but only a few received the e-mail address and even less got the web address.
- Video files are always large, and it took a long time to send

a video between phones – not to mention the time to figure out how to do it. So much for that idea!

- I tested my idea on a few close friends. Even though using Bluetooth is simple, most of them didn't know how to use it to receive contact information, and they were also resistant to having me explain it to them. I didn't want this to occur with any new contacts so I thought I'd better find a different solution.

In the end, I decided that using Bluetooth had some pros:

- It's great for sharing names and phone numbers (and hands free accessories).
- It saved me from waiting for my new contact to enter my name into their new phone.

And some cons:

- It was not good for sharing video
- It failed consistently to send complete contact information (that is E-mail address, web address) to other phones.

I eventually decided to keep the Bluetooth alternative in my back pocket and continued searching.

Later I saw that all cell phones consistently do an excellent job of sending information in the form of simple text messages. It also seems like most people are comfortable communicating with texts. Then I had a major break through. I noticed that most cell phones can "sense" phone numbers, e-mail addresses and web addresses included in text messages. To see what I mean go to your phone and select "options" while viewing a text message. The phone will prompt you to save these details, walk you through the process, and even *offer to go to a web address*! The only catch is that you have to sign up for web service on your cellular plan to view web sites. Add to this, YouTube is free and videos uploaded to their site will play on just about any web enabled phone. That's when I realized I'd discovered a wicked little widget for self-promoting. With this in mind, I devised a solid step-by-step method to include cell phones in your mix of delivery devices for self-promoting:

1. Prepare an introductory video about yourself as I described earlier. Feel free to use mine as a model and reference. Your video must be 10 minutes or less (I'll explain why in step 3) but should ideally be between 3 and 5 minutes. I recommend using iMovie for this.

2. When finished, log on to www.YouTube.com and sign up for a free account.

3. Upload your video to the site. If you use iMovie, you can take advantage of the built in YouTube feature to do this. You should also use the space provided by YouTube for the video description to introduce yourself as well as the video. YouTube will reject videos longer than 10 minutes.

4. Once your video uploads, wait for YouTube to process it and make it available for viewing. When it's available, click on the title of your video to play it. While it's

playing, copy the URL in the address window of your browser.

5. Make sure your cell service plan includes web surfing to avoid any extra charges. Encourage others to do the same. Enable the media player on your phone. Refer to your phone's user manual if you need help.

6. Go to your phone and find where you can create your own "Preset Text Message". ("Preset Text Message" is specific to Sprint. AT&T and T-Mobile phones call it a "Text Template", and Verizon Wireless phones call it a "Quick Text".) This is just a plain text message that stays stored on your phone and ready to send. Refer to the user manual for your phone if you need help.

7. Compose your message with your name, phone number, e-mail address, and the URL for the video you just uploaded. Don't worry about spaces between the area code and phone number prefix. Your message should be fewer than 100 characters including spaces. Here's mine:

Mel Brown 1234567890 melbass@aol.com see/hear now at http://www.youtube.com/watch?v=WBwoUZ2RqN8

8. Take some time to practice entering names, numbers and e-mail addresses into your phone. Learn how

to find and send your saved message quickly. Get good and blazing fast at it! Practice by sending the message to your own phone, e-mail, or friends e-mail addresses.

9. The next time someone asks for your number, say something like "Sure. Let me get yours too." Quickly enter their name and number into your phone and immediately send them your saved message. Then ask for their e-mail address and send the text there, too.

10. Tell your new contact that you've emailed them your contact info and make sure they received your text message. Then let them know that if they can surf the web on their phone, they can see and hear you now by opening your text message, selecting "options" and choosing the URL in your message.

11. If the new contacts phone is web enabled, you'll enjoy blowing them away with your readiness. They'll be able to see your video on their phone and read a brief description of the video and you. They'll also be able to add your information to their address book with minimal effort.

12. Another great benefit of using this technique is that your new contact can show or forward your text to someone else and so on. Let your new contact

know they can save the URL for the video by "book marking" the page in their phone's web browser. They can also forward the page from their phones' browser menu too. Congratulations! You've just turned your new contact into a believer and a good sales agent of your skills!

The Internet

This includes my web site, MySpace, and YouTube pages. Let's face it; if you don't occupy a spot on the Internet, you're doing your business and your career a disservice. The Internet gives anyone almost anywhere in the world 24 hours a day, 7 days a week, 365 days of the year an opportunity to see you perform. This fact alone should be enough incentive for you to get your web presence together when you consider how hard it is to distinguish yourself from others and to contact potential clients. Not taking advantage of MySpace and YouTube is inexcusable because they're free. I've worked for people who I've never met face-to-face as a direct result of them being able to get to know me and my playing through my Internet presence. Living in a major city was once a prerequisite in the music business. These days, a musician can spend some time in a major music city while building a reputation as a player and making contacts, then move anywhere and preserve those relationships with the Internet. The mechanics of building a web site or MySpace page is beyond the scope of this book, but I can offer a couple of tips:

The first program I learned for making web sites was Dreamweaver MX. It's a cool and powerful program, but the learning curve was a bit steep for me. I bought an excellent "Training from the Source" book online (It came with a trial version of the program.) and worked through it for about a week. I soon realized that using this program regularly would involve a lot more time, study, and effort than I was willing to commit. I didn't want to be an expert at web design, but I did want a site that I could quickly build and maintain myself. If you want to build a web site fast and don't know anything about doing it, stop by an Apple Store and try iWeb. I'll be hosting a web site for this book at www.fromzerotosideman.com beginning in mid 2008. I'm building the site on a Mac using iWeb. If neither one of these choices is for you, I suggest that you pay someone to get your web presence happening.

So, now that you have a great demo, all that remains is for you to introduce yourself as the new 'Killer' in town. If you've already been in your town awhile, you can take advantage of a standing opportunity available to anyone at anytime: to redefine yourself as the 'Killer' no one knew about! This is like seeing an old friend after a few years and noticing that they've dropped twenty pounds, gotten into shape, and have started a new life. The process of getting a positive word out about yourself and your service is called self-promotion, and I'll talk about that now.

SELF-PROMOTE

Self-promoting is simply advertising and marketing yourself to others. It's the act of getting a positive word into the musical community about your business and your character. Self-promoting is a numbers game with a singular purpose: to make as many people aware of you and your service as possible. The more people who know, the more potential there is to be working. It's that simple.

So Why Doesn't Every Musician Self-Promote?

Many musicians view self-promotion as difficult, awkward, tedious, unnecessary, or uncomfortable and just won't do it at all. Other musicians are just lazy or have no clue about how to self-promote. Some musicians make excuses for not self-promoting. They give me a good chuckle when they make comments like

- "I don't like to blow my own horn."

- "I prefer to let my playing do the talking."

- "If people want me, they know where to find me."

- "I'd do a great job if people would just call me!"

All of these are just excuses for not taking care of business. A good friend gave me an old saying to remember about excuses, and it goes like this: "Excuses are like a** holes, everybody has one, and they all stink!" Now here are a few important reasons that you *should* self-promote as Sideman:

1 – Spreading the Word Should Never Stop

When I was talking about Choosing the Life, I said that being a Sideman is the same as starting your own small business, right? Go turn on your television or radio. Every fifteen minutes or so, the show that you're watching or listening to takes a commercial break. Notice who makes these commercials? Listerine, Scope, Tylenol, Viagra, Kleenex, Pepsi, Coke, Snickers, Bubble Yum, Barbie, Apple Computers, Kraft Macaroni and Cheese, Allstate Insurance, Charles Schwab, Smith Barney, H&R Block, Mercedes-Benz, Audi, Ford, Chevrolet, Toyota, Band-Aid, Xerox, Nike, *Monday Night Football*, Outback Steakhouse, McDonald's, Burger King, Taco Bell, Wal-Mart, *The New York Times*, *The Wall Street Journal*, Johnson's Baby Shampoo, and the list goes on, and on, and on.

Although you could choose any of these names to show my point, I'll use Wal-Mart for my example. According to Wal-Mart's web site, Wal-Mart has been around since 1962 (over 45 years), employs 1.9 million people, has over 4,000 stores in the US, and 2,900 stores in 14 other countries. It seems to me that everyone should know what Wal-Mart is by now, right? Everyone should also know what they sell and where they are by now, yet there's still a direct correlation between how much Wal-Mart advertises and how much business they do. More advertising, business goes up. Less advertising, business goes down. Keep these facts in mind, and then ask yourself a simple question:

If Wal-Mart still has to advertise, why shouldn't I?

The same applies to Apple Computer Company. The iPod is the number one selling MP3 player in the world. Yet Apple still spends millions of dollars on TV and radio advertising to spread the word to people about the iPod and the service it provides to its users. Why is my business any different? As a Sideman, I have to advertise my business — just like Wal-Mart, Apple Computer Company, and the rest of those companies I mentioned.

2 –   People (Including Your Friends) Need and Want Reassurance of Your Interest.

Don't make the mistake of thinking that you'll eventually get to a level where you won't have to self-promote. I have a successful career and I'm well-known in my city, but I constantly remind previous and potential clients that I'm not too busy, too expensive, or uninterested in working with them. There is nothing wrong with being proactive to keep the phone ringing and business coming in — that's why I do it all the time. I can only speak for myself, but I'd rather get a call and have to turn an offer for work down than to not get a call at all.

3 – You're Responsible for Other's Views of You.

I remember telling a bass player friend of mine in LA that I'd just turned down a well-paid, high-profile gig with a very hot blonde singer/actress named Jessica — and the gig was still available. He seemed excited but finished the conversation with, "Can you have them call me later today? I'm taking a nap." Now if this friend had been a successful Sideman, I might have understood his need to get some rest. But he'd just moved to town, wasn't working, was struggling to meet his expenses, and had asked me the day before if he could sleep on my couch for "a few days or until I can get a gig."

I ended the call and immediately reached out to Friend #2 whose first question was, "Do you have a contact number and a name? I'd like to see what I can do to make this happen!" That night, Friend #2 called me back to thank me, to tell that he'd gotten hired, and that he was headed to rehearse for a TV appearance with Jessica. The next day I checked my messages, and Friend #1 was on my voice mail. He seemed genuinely confused that he didn't get the call — which was his for the taking if he'd handled his business! His message went something like this, "Hey, man, I haven't heard anything from those people. Did you give them my number? I'm about to get something to eat, but it'll only take a couple of hours. Tell them to keep trying if I don't pick up!" After seven years in LA, this guy still hasn't landed a gig and is planning to leave, because, in his words, "No one's calling me for work." — Go figure!

As I said in the previous chapter, you're going to be introducing or redefining yourself to the musical community in your area, so now is a great time to learn that self-promoting as a Sideman has three unique sides:

1. Distributing your demo and contact information, maintaining a web presence, and seeking out opportunities where others can check you out in person.

2. Maintaining a reliable "network" of music industry contacts.

3. Endorsements.

The first two sides are equally important. I think one without the other is useless. Endorsements are optional. I'll talk about each one of these sides in-depth, but before I do, I recommend checking out a must-see video on the Musician's Institute web site:

http://www.mi.edu/video.aspx?vid=9

Musician's Institute is a great music school in Los Angeles, and this video is an outstanding introduction to networking in the music industry. It contains ideas for starting a conversation, how and when to enter an existing conversation, and exiting a conversation. It contains some great information about body language and most importantly, tips about topics of conversation. There are several other relevant topics discussed here, and you'll be doing yourself an enormous favor by watching it. The speaker, Mr. Dan Kimpel, does an outstanding job addressing a much-needed but rarely-taught skill in our business. Make sure that you watch it, because it'll only help to get you ready to give out your demo. Alrighty then! Let's walk on to the track and get ready to win in the big rat race...

On Your Mark . . .

If you're moving to a major music city, I recommend having 300-500 of copies of your demo professionally done with your name and web address printed on the front. (Don't print your phone number on the CD, because it may change!) You may think that's too many demos, but trust me, in a city like LA, you'll go through these quickly. If you need to do a few discs at a time, say 20 or so, I'd burn the discs myself and take advantage of HP's LightScribe technology to keep the look professional. Another option is to hire a local company to do a "short run" of at least 150 discs.

Business cards are easy to make at home now, but professional printers are advertising attractive cheap prices too. I think a standard business card with just a name, a number, and what instrument you play is simply a waste of time. I have a stack of business cards given to me by various people. I can't remember where I met them, if they were cool, if they're talented, or if I even want to contact them again. These cards all contain the information that most business cards should, but they also have a feature that no business card should have — a blank side. If you're going to take the time and make the effort handing out business cards, why not use all the space available on the card to communicate something and to help them remember you? In a city like LA, everyone is constantly networking. Everyone meets several people everyday, and you should expect to be forgotten a few times. That's why I use a business card with a photo on one side and my contact information (name, instrument, e-mail address, web site, and phone number) on the other side. I want to give a new contact every opportunity to remember me. Anyone asking for a card gets a demo with two business cards. Those who already have a demo get my business card. I don't print my business cards at home because I can get 1000 of them printed cheaply by a professional and save my printer for more important jobs. I deliver my profile CD in a small, sealed CD envelope with a clear window and two business cards inside.

Get Set...

Make sure that you have a solid system to collect, organize, store, and protect your new contact's information. If you've built a web site, it's time to find a host and get it uploaded onto the web. If you know nothing about web hosting and want a user-friendly introduction to it, go to an Apple Store and ask one of the folks to explain it to you. Once your site is up, you'll be advertising your services worldwide and be reachable by e-mail 24/7/365. Nice!

Next, it's time to make sure that your Myspace and YouTube pages are up and running. Finally, let's start distributing your demo to others. Here's a list of twelve moves to make when you hit the pavement self-promoting.

Go!

1 – Sit In (A.K.A. the "Live Demo")

Live and in the flesh is a great way to show others who you are and how you play. Go to every place that you visited and see every band you saw while you were making your Master List of songs. Make sure you review your notes on who was playing, what gear they were using, how they were dressed, who was in charge, etc. Then show up dressed appropriately and ready to wreck the joint. When the band takes a break, say hi to the Bandleader and the band, and let them know that you'd like to sit in sometime. I'd always say something like, "I'm trying to get started here in town, and I'd like to give you my demo and get your number. Everything you need to know is on the demo including some videos and stuff. Would that be cool with you all? I already know all of the tunes — you won't have to rehearse me." Then I'd say something like this to the bass player, "I'm not trying to take any work from you or do anything uncool. LA is a big city with a lot of great players. I'm new here, and I'm trying to introduce myself to the scene. I'm just trying to make sure the people I meet remember me the first time. Congratulations on being here and having a gig, man!" Be honest and be genuine. In a city like LA, the players understand. If you're fake and insincere, people can tell and they won't trust you.

Remember what I said about learning songs? Well, this is the first place where it pays off. You should be as prepared as possible before you sit in, and practice good "Sit-In Etiquette". In other words, you should:

- know all the songs that a band is doing before you ever ask to sit in, and

- be able to immediately suggest several songs in their repertoire you'd like to play. Don't be the idiot that gets invited on stage to sit in but when asked to choose a tune says "I dunno. What do you want to play?"

- Get your axe, horn, sticks, or whatever ready BEFORE you get invited to the stage. Don't make everyone wait for you or cause unnecessary "Dead Air" while you tune up (remember that tuner?), pull out your drum key, empty your spit valve, or practice your fast licks.

- Assume they're only going to let you play one song or *maybe* two if you sound good. Don't wait for them to ask you to leave.

- Remember that this is a great opportunity to show everyone that you can walk in and slam even though the conditions aren't perfect.

When you're done, make sure that each one of the musicians gets your demo, gives you their contact information, then thank them all and head for the next spot. Do this until you've covered all the bands on your list. Some of them will let you play and hear you right there — which should lead to new friends and maybe some more work. Some of them won't. But all of them will hear and see your demo, and that's what matters here.

Now, before I go on, I have to make absolutely sure that you understand something. When you show up somewhere handing out demos and asking to sit in, you're putting yourself in the hot seat. If you haven't taken care of business in the 'Educating Yourself' department, you'll immediately become "That jerk who showed up running his mouth, handing out demos, but couldn't play." The only justification you have for showing up and trying to make room for yourself this way is that your skills are together, and all of these folks stand to benefit from your presence in town. If you cut corners up to this point, you'll pay for it here.

After you hit up all the folks who play the music you know and love, add up all your songs and see who you are again. Go to the free paper and find the bands that play some of your newly developed styles. Follow those same instructions for sitting in and giving out your demo to all of these players, too. Don't bother if you know less than 250 songs in any style. You won't sound good, or you'll get caught not knowing a tune and regret it later. Once you've exhausted your genres, you should look for open jam sessions where your strong genres are being played and again follow the sitting in and distribution instructions.

The only downside to sitting in is that you may not be performing material relevant to a specific client. The manager of a Country singer hanging out at the Reggae club where you're sitting in is an example of this. This is why you should always have copies of your demo with you. If someone in the audience asks you for your business card, you'll have the opportunity to turn a good first impression into a great one by handing them a first-class demo. And, by the way, just because you *can* sit in doesn't mean you have to or even should. Why? Because you only get one chance to make a first impression — so you should make it count! If you're not going to enjoy it, sound good, or increase your opportunities, then why do it? I won't sit in if the bass player's amplifier sucks or if it's a brand that I don't know how to use. I won't sit in if the sound is bad in the room. I also make it a general rule to play my own bass when sitting in, because different players set up their instruments differently. These differences can lead to you being uncomfortable, or being unable to perform as well as you would on your own instrument. Once you've done some legwork and gotten your demo into circulation, you'll want to follow up with the people who you gave your demo to.

2 –   Be a Great Sub

Find all the players who play the same styles as you, because much of your work will come from other players who play your instrument. Everyone's constantly trying to get to something better, but they don't want to burn any bridges when new opportunities happen. New opportunities always come at the most inconvenient time and under the worst circumstances. One way to keep things cool with bandleaders is to send a sub who does a great job. Being a great sub is a solid way to get into the scene and advance quickly. You'll be an excellent sub if you followed the instructions in this book.

3 – Find the General Business Agents

If you're a reader, you should find all the General Business bandleaders in town now. It's difficult to sit in at General Business gigs. You're going to have to ask if you can come down and audition for them, if they'll check you out on the web, or if you can send them your demo and follow up in a few days. General Business bandleaders are always looking for players, and if you know all the songs that they play and have strong reading skills, they'll put you to work immediately.

4 – Find the Churches that Pay Musicians.

You should contact every church of your denomination and then all the nondenominational churches as well. Ask to speak with the Pastor of Music and how you could best introduce them to your service.

5 – Hit the Rehearsal Spots.

If you're in a major music city, you should learn where all the rehearsal spots are. Major tours can rehearse for up to a month before they go out on the road, and these are great places to see what will be expected of you if you land one of these gigs. You can also get a feel for which musicians work together often and the gigs they get the most. Don't call the rehearsal space, because the employees are told not to give out any information on the phone. You've got to be real cool hanging out around these places — like — blend into the wallpaper cool. Rich and Famous Artists are sensitive to who is in the room, and their overzealous handlers are always looking for an opportunity to prove their loyalty by telling some uninvited schmuck to leave. If you see an opportunity to hand out your demo here, do it, but do it discreetly.

6 – Find the MDs.

"MD" means Musical Director in the music industry. MDs are the people onstage in charge of the band that is backing up Artists. MDs often finish a tour or gig and immediately get offered a similar position somewhere else, so they're always looking for players.

7 – Find the Struggling Artists.

Struggling Artists are always looking for players also. Find a few talented but struggling Artists who you like, and forge relationships with them. Commit to helping them when you can. In this business, you never know who is going to be the next hot flavor of the month. If the Artist does any recording, you may be able to add this material to your demo or web site as latest news or extra quality content.

8 – Find the Agencies that Book Sidelining Gigs.

You never know when one of these gigs could land you next to a popular Superstar in a blockbuster film, and the hype can't hurt. Find these folks, ask them how to present your stuff, and follow up.

9 – Go to the "Cattle Calls".

These are auditions that just about anyone can show up to in major music cities. I'd always show up to these to hand out my demo, not necessarily to get the gig. But hey! Anything can happen!

10 – Find the Contractors.

Contractors (Union and nonunion) hire musicians or put bands together for tours, shows, sessions, and so on. They're always looking for reliable players, so make sure they get your demo, and then follow up.

11 – Go Through the CD Credits.

Note the Sidemen playing on the project, find them on the Internet, and then try to get your demo to them or their management. Invite them to your MySpace or YouTube page. A great player is a great player no matter where they live or where they're from. This is a great way to contact some Sidemen who are already working. If you have anything to offer, they'll recognize you and possibly throw you a bone. Don't worry about your location, because in this business anything can happen. I got a call from a friend on tour with Michael Bolton. Their regular bass player (an excellent player named Schuyler Deale) had some emergency happen and had to return home for a couple of days. They were calling me to see if I was in Arizona at the time, because it was their next stop and they needed someone to cover the gig.

12 – Take a Chance on the Impossible.

I got my first "Big Break" by sending a video to Arsenio Hall and asking him to let me sit in with his band. Guess what? He did.

Networking

A "network" is a selection of individuals you choose to share information and maintain regular contact with in the industry. "Networking" is the process of meeting people and exchanging contact information for that purpose. This is an invaluable survival skill, because a solid network can provide a pathway to new work opportunities and help you stay informed about current events. In other words, your network gives you eyes and ears where you're not physically present. Here are three ways that networking helped my own career:

1. The most desirable gigs are rarely advertised. Someone looking to fill a desirable position usually starts by asking a trusted friend to recommend someone. That trusted friend can strengthen existing relationships and further their own career by recommending a winner. This was the case when I heard from a drummer on my network (an excellent player in LA named Land Richards) that Gladys Knight was looking for a bass player. Land provided me with a name and a contact number for Benjamin Wright, who was the Musical Director for Knight at the time, but it was up to me to follow it up. If you'd like to hear how I did, log on here and you can hear the story from Benjamin himself:

   http://www.melbrown.net/word-of-mouth.php?wid=8

   Keep in mind that I'd never met Benjamin, or anyone else in the band. My network and my demo got me in the door there. Another example was when Gladys decided to do an extended engagement at the Flamingo Hilton in Las Vegas. I didn't want to spend that much time in "Lost Wages" so I started calling folks on my network to see if anything else was happening. A contractor named Bruce Sterling told me that Marc Anthony would be making a change and that I'd be great for the gig if I were available. Bruce was working closely with a consultant for Sony Records named Chris Apostle. Bruce showed Chris my demo and then I met Chris for a handshake and to say hello. Three days after leaving Knight's organization, I was on a plane to New York to begin rehearsing for Marc's HBO Special and US Tour.

2.   If you're currently working, your network can lead you to added opportunities. While I was on the road with Gladys, I heard from a friend and audio engineer on my network named Phil Magnotti. He told me that Chuck Loeb was going to be recording his new CD. A quick check of my schedule revealed that I was going to be an hour outside New York City at the same time. I called Chuck and said that I'd be in town and would love to play if he could use me. Chuck said it was cool, and we booked the date. I rented a car, drove down to the city, and recorded two tracks on his CD called *The Moon, The Stars and the Setting Sun*. One of the tracks called "Beneath the Light" made it to #2 on the radio charts, which in turn led to other recording opportunities.

3.   You can benefit from others' experiences. Anything that you want to do, someone has probably already tried it or something similar. I'll offer an example here, too. I remember a cool singer named Julie Ragins called me and asked if I'd like to do a sidelining gig she knew about. She'd seen the on-camera stuff on my demo and thought of me for a hot opportunity happening that week. I said yes, and Julie took some time to tell me about the guy who was hiring musicians,

"He doesn't like people that talk a lot; he admires patience, sharp musicianship, and he's a real by-the-book, union guy. Make sure that you bring a passport, and fill out the paperwork before you get there." She passed my number along, and I also reached out to the contractor. I followed her advice to the letter. The gig turned out to be a two-day engagement — the first day was recording a cover version of "One In A Million" an old Larry Graham hit ballad. We worked at a nice West LA studio. The second day was standing two feet from Eddie Murphy while he sang that song to Janet Jackson for the wedding scene in the *Nutty Professor II: The Klumps*. I actually got some camera time in the movie, and I still use the clip on my website for self-promoting. Julie's advice was right on the money, because she had worked for this guy before, and I benefited from her experience.

I hope these examples make my point clear. You can see that to be effective your contacts need to be inspired to stay in touch with you. The inspiration to stay in touch with you should come from your demo and from other's experiences with you. Everyone knows that high-quality people are the first to hear about opportunities. If you've done a good job of Choosing the Life, Equipping Yourself, Educating Yourself, and Making a Demo, you should start hearing about new opportunities from the people on your network soon after you start building one. I'd suggest trying to build and maintain a solid local network of at least 75 music-industry professionals who know you, know your playing, your interests, your other skills, and your ambitions as a Sideman. Notice that I didn't say "75 Musicians". In this business, anyone close to a great opportunity can throw your name into the hat.

Endorsements

A lot of musicians misunderstand endorsements and how they relate to self-promotion. I've met several young musicians who claim to "be endorsed by Company So-and-So". It's as if "Company So-and-So" is vouching for the musicians' abilities instead of the player vouching for the quality of the company's product. Too many ignorant musicians mistakenly look at this "Company approval" as being the purpose of an endorsement relationship, and they miss what they could gain by having one. Remember:

Products Don't Vouch for Musicians — Musicians Vouch for Products!

Endorsement relationships happen when companies believe they can increase product sales by attaching a well-respected or successful person's name and likeness to it. Look at Michael Jordan for example. Do you think he's the greatest basketball player alive because he wears Nike Shoes, Hanes Underwear, and eats a certain hot dog? I don't think so! I'd bet all of my basses that Jordan would dunk on you just the same if he wore a G-String from Victoria's

Secret, a pair of old Pumas, with any hot dog stuck between his cheek and gums! The fact is that Michael vouches for Nike's shoes, not the other way around. Michael vouches for Hanes underwear, not the other way around. And here's the clincher: He's PAID WELL to vouch for these products! These companies pay Michael Jordan handsomely to be seen with their products and to say that they're great. Instrument makers should pay you to do the same. Of course, Nike and Hanes are much bigger than X Instrument maker, so asking for millions is not practical. But asking the company to name a model after you and paying you a royalty for every instrument sold is reasonable. If you're not famous enough to warrant an Artist model, you should be open to compensation in some other way. At the least, a company should be willing to provide you with a few instruments, repair services, and exposure of some kind. What you're willing to accept is up to you — but you should be compensated in some way for your endorsement of any products. Endorsements can be a great way to gain exposure but should be equally considered as a way to lower your cost of doing business and increasing your bottom line. Let me make this clear too: An endorsement does not confirm your ability to play, it only proves that someone believes that more units can be sold if your name is attached to it. While I'm on this topic, I may as well share with you how I got my endorsements:

I got my first endorsement before I ever got on a tour or moved away from Denver. I liked these strings called Dean Markley SR2000s, but they were expensive and hard to find. Most of the dealers in town were happy to order them for me, but they'd always try to charge me the full price — around $45 per set. Then I decided to do something about it. I'd learned the basics of putting a bio together and presenting it to companies from a bassist in Denver called Michael Friedman. Michael played in a popular group called Dotsero, and after securing an endorsement with a bass company, he gave me some pointers on pursuing endorsements for myself. I followed his advice but added my own twist. When I submitted my stuff to Dean Markley, I told them that they had absolutely no presence in Denver and that I could help them change that. I told them that it was great that Will Lee was using their strings and had his own signature set but that he wasn't available to answer any questions for us in Denver. I told them that I was an up-and-coming player and that I would bust my ass to help them move more strings in Denver for one year. In exchange, they'd sell me the strings at a large discount. If I was successful, they'd give me a full endorsement — if not, I'd go back to paying full price like everyone else. They agreed — I succeeded — and I've endorsed Dean Markley strings for almost 15 years now.

So that's the story with Self-Promoting. The only thing left is to go to work. Now I'll share some thoughts that should be helpful to you at this stage of the game.

...TO SIDEMAN (TIME TO GO TO WORK!)

You might already know this, but I'll say it anyway: Be on time, in tune, and ready to play. Leave your problems, angst, negativity, excuses, bad attitude, and all other issues at the door. There's no place for this crap at the gig.

Set your mind to take care of the business at hand and nothing else. Before I let you go, I'll share some closing thoughts about why all Sidemen get called, what to expect on your new gigs, and keeping it together as a newbie.

Why Did They Call...?

Okay... so you've done all of this work getting educated, learning songs, making a tricked-out demo, and then you heard that some other guy just got hired for some gig and you didn't. As a Sideman, you'll have to learn to keep the din of "There's-a-new-musician-in-town-flavor-of-the-month" talk, or the "Oh, my God, have you heard so-and-so" hubbub in perspective. It's just talk. Remember that you can't be all things to all people, and *neither can they*. We'd all like to get calls because of our great looks, our outstanding musicianship, our creative genius, and our fantastic demo, but the reality is that most calls come because of some other "less than glamorous circumstance".

The truth is that every Sideman in the music industry gets called for work for pretty much the same set of reasons. I made a list of some of these reasons for you:

- **First Call Gigs** — These calls come because you are the player of choice or referred by the player of choice for a performance or project. Being the player of choice means less scrutiny, more creative license, and a little more job security. These calls come from people who have heard about you, were impressed by your demo, or have seen you perform. They've usually decided that working with you could have long-term advantages. Don't confuse "First Call" with "First-Class". You could be considered the first call Sideman for a gig playing next to an open landfill with "Stank and the Garbage Men"! There are always other great players lurking, so don't take it personally if you didn't get it this time.

- **Sub Gigs** — These are calls for you to cover a gig because the regular player is planning to be absent from a scheduled performance. These calls will usually come from the regular player or the MD, but I've received calls like this from just about every other possible person associated with a particular gig. These calls are a great opportunity to show that you can prepare and perform as well as the first-call guy. I specialized in subbing when I first moved to LA. I scored a steady gig when I first got to town, so when I wasn't on the road, I stayed working by becoming an excellent sub for as many gigs as possible. Being a sub on a gig is considered temporary, and it's understood that you are "subbing" not "auditioning". It's not cool to try to steal a gig that you're subbing on, so don't do it. You can't help it if you become the preferred player though. Just be honest and keep everything on the table so you don't look like a jerk.

- **Clean Up Gigs** – These are calls to replace someone who's not performing or behaving as expected on a gig. There are no limits to what reasons, circumstances, or events can lead to a call like this. I've been the "clean up guy" for players who were alcoholics, drug addicts, lazy musicians, bullies onstage, Jazz snobs, racists, thieves, musically incompatible, or just plain socially inept. When folks on the gig have had enough, the Artist or management will choose a time when a smooth transition can happen and begin discreetly grooming a replacement behind the scenes. These calls can be tough, because they want you to be silent about the change until you start the gig, and you might even know the person being replaced. If you exhibit any of those negative characteristics I just mentioned on the gig, I might be the "clean up guy" for you…

- **Emergency Gigs** – These are gigs that come about because of last minute and totally unexpected situations. Sudden death, family emergencies, baby deliveries, accidents, acts of God, and even someone thinking they won the lottery and blowing off the gig have all led to me getting emergency calls.

- **Goodwill Gigs** – These are gigs that you do as a favor for a friend or someone else to "get your foot in the door" or to strengthen a relationship. This is done by lowering your fee or by taking money out of the equation altogether. Do this sparingly! You don't want the word to get around that you're an easy target to ask for discounted or free services.

- **Social Gigs** – Although musicianship is always important, there are gigs that come about simply because you have friends in the band. These gigs are convenient because you can enjoy a "First Call" feeling, but these gigs mostly come because the folks in the band like hanging with you on the road or something. They think that you "fit in" with them socially. There's nothing wrong with getting a gig this way, but I'd avoid making this social acceptance a requirement. Plan to work with folks who you know on a "pleasantly professional" basis the most.

- **Down the List Gigs** – These are gigs that come to you because the bandleader has exhausted his list of preferred players and is actively looking for anyone who can cover the gig.

- **Exploitative Gigs** — These are gigs that come from shady characters looking to get your service free. You'd be surprised at how often it happens in this business, even to veteran players. You can avoid being taken advantage of in this way by asking about the money in advance and not agreeing to the work until a satisfactory agreement is made. And speaking of money...

Always Ask About the Money!

If your phone is ringing, that means it's time to do business. That business is delivering a service for a reasonable fee to as many clients as possible, period. It's always great to be creative and add something to the music, but a lot of being a Sideman is just playing the part. The devil is in the details here — about the gig and the dough. Anyone calling Mel Brown for work is asked about the money. If a friend calls me, they should describe what the gig pays out of respect. If I'm speaking to a new and unfamiliar client, I set a precedent for clear communication about the money at the beginning. I'll say something like, "I appreciate you thinking of me for this project and it sounds like fun. We've never done business before, and I need to know how much this project pays, who is responsible for paying me, what form will that pay be (check, cash, rubles, etc.) and when should I expect payment." When you walk into McDonald's, is the price of a Big Mac a secret? Nope! It's posted on the wall where everyone can see it. You may have to look a bit harder to find the prices at an upscale restaurant, but they're there for you to see before you order. The same should be true in your business. Don't post your fees on the web, but do make sure to discuss them with your clients before you start work.

Every now and then you'll get an opportunity to get into a gig at the beginning, but most of the time, you'll be walking into an established gig as the "newbie". Being the newbie can be difficult if you don't know what to expect. I'll share some things that you can look out for:

Social Behavior 101: Bullies, Caretakers, and Busybodies

Being on a gig is the same as being in a small social group, and all the rules for group behavior and "norms" apply here. You're going to learn quickly that all behaviors on the gig don't reflect high professional standards. When you're new on a gig, the fact that you don't know the ropes can lead to some interesting interactions with some of the other players.

- Bullies on the gig are musicians who try to intimidate you onstage and off by giving the impression that they control the show and influence whether you keep the gig or not. They're usually the "lifers" on a given gig. They've gotten too comfortable and feel above reproach. Bullies have poor boundaries, and have low social standards. I've had bullies try to tell me what to play onstage in front of the audience. I've had them keep an inside joke going at my expense or make any mistakes on my part the topic of conversation in front of the Artist or the rest of the group. The best way to deal with an onstage bully is to set up communication with the MD in front of the band before the show and confirm that you'll be taking all of your directions from them only. How you deal with a bully offstage is up to you. I'll usually send a nicely wrapped gift box of fresh road kill or some black roses to the bully's room.

- Caretakers are musicians who do their jobs well, mind their own business, and are also very professional. Caretakers will sometimes try to help newbie's succeed by shepherding them though learning the gig. Be cool to these folks and express your appreciation by buying them lunch or a cup of coffee. Caretakers always know what's happening with the current gig and many others. Follow their lead as much as possible.

- Busybodies are the noisemakers and gossips on the gig. They're usually talking about other people's business or trying to find out more about someone else's business, all the while claiming to be appalled by other's indulgence in these activities. Steer clear of these folks unless you like drama.

Different is Just Different

The biggest challenge you'll face as a newbie is surviving the period of time the band needs to adjust to your different sound and playing style. Excellent musicians understand, accept, and embrace the difference. Mediocre players, on the other hand, hear the difference in a negative way and react to it by trying to "fix you". Here are some comments made to me as a newbie:

- "Well, [enter previous player's name here] played it this way…"

- "I know you're playing what's on the CD, but try something else that [enter famous musicians name here] or [enter famous musicians name here] might play."

- "You're not playing that right. I've been on this gig for xx years, and I know when it's being played right."

The best way to handle these situations is to know the songs so well and be so musically authentic that anyone would have second thoughts about challenging you at all. Authenticity trumps all here. Your second best defense is to have clear communication with the MD and establish that you'll be taking your direction from them only. For others trying to direct you, carefully decide if you're being disrespected (Bully), helped (Caretaker), or just interfered with (Busybody), and respond accordingly. You might want to practice some polite ways to tell someone to mind their own business if necessary. Remember that different is just different, not necessarily worse. The band will eventually adjust to the way you play it. You should only worry if you're not very good and then a real player shows everyone how it should sound.

It's like that, Sideman. That's most of what you need to know to get this thing on and crackin'. The rest you'll have to learn from your own experiences as you progress. You need to know that the industry is shrinking; Big Tours are happening less; CD sales for Artists are down, and recording budgets are smaller. It's harder than ever to make a name as a session musician, because the trend is toward programmed or sampled music and self-contained bands now. Building a successful career in the way that some players have, such as Ricky Lawson, Gregg Phillinganes, Nathan East, Vinnie Colaiuta, Marcus Miller, Will Lee, Brent Mason, Dan Huff, Steve Lukather, Paul Jackson, or Steve Gadd, is rare — but not impossible. As you can see, any number of factors can impact your "getting over" as much as your skill set or qualifications. All you can do is prepare yourself for success. Choose this Life with your eyes open. Equip Yourself with the right tools. Educate Yourself about your craft and become skillful on your instrument. Make a Demo of your skills that the world can see. Then Self-Promote as much as possible. After you've done these things to the best of your ability, there's nothing left except to enjoy the ride. Get your thick skin on for those fools who reject you, and always deliver your very best to those who don't.

See you at the gig!
Mel

CPSIA information can be obtained
at www.ICGtesting.com
Printed in the USA
LVHW090129090421
683964LV00007B/240